I have found in the Bible
plenty of evidence that God
has guided people. I find,
too, assurance that he is willing to guide me. He has
been at it for a long time.
His hand reaches toward me.
I have only to take it. . . .

This is a book about the
guidance of God, but it is
not six easy lessons on how
to get it. It is a collection
of observations from per-
sonal experience and from
the Bible on why and how
God does, in fact, guide his
children.

Elisabeth Elliot

Also by Elisabeth Elliot

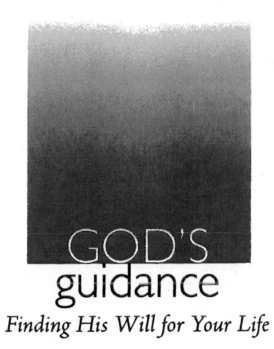

GOD'S
guidance

Finding His Will for Your Life

Second Edition
with STUDY GUIDE

Elisabeth Elliot

Revell
Grand Rapids, Michigan

© 1973, 1992, 1997 by Elisabeth Elliot

Published by Fleming H. Revell
a division of Baker Publishing Group
P.O. Box 6287, Grand Rapids, MI 49516-6287

New paperback edition published 2006

Previously published in 1973 by Word Books under the title *A Slow and Certain Light*

Printed in the United States of America

Library of Congress Cataloging-in-Publication Data

Elliot, Elisabeth.
      God's guidance : finding his will for your life / Elisabeth Elliot.—2nd ed. / with study guide.
         p. cm.
      Includes bibliographical references.
      ISBN 10: 0-8007-3133-6 (pbk.)
      ISBN 978-0-8007-3133-5 (pbk.)
      1. Christian life. 2. Providence and government of God. 3. God—Will. I. Title.
BV4501.3.E452 2006
248.4—dc22   2006000439

To Van
(Eleanor C. Vandevort)
who has been
a witness to my life
and who once told me that
following God is not like
walking a tightrope

contents

While corn is springing from the earth above,
what lies beneath is raked over like a fire,
and out of its rocks comes lapis lazuli,
dusted with flecks of gold.
No bird of prey knows the way there,
and the falcon's keen eye cannot descry it. . . .
Where then does wisdom come from,
and where is the source of understanding? . . .
God understands the way to it,
he alone knows its source;
for he can see to the ends of the earth
and he surveys everything under heaven.

Job 28:5–7, 20, 23, 24 NEB

If any man will do his will, he shall know. . . .

John 7:17

introduction

The desire for instant advice is not new. Sorcerers, magicians, wise men, oracles, witch doctors, palmists, shamans, astrologers, and fortune-tellers of all kinds have always been in business. The continuing sale of books and magazines on "horoscopy" and astrology and the growth of professional counseling and guidance services (not to mention computer dating agencies) indicate that although more education for more people is available than ever before, the majority seem to feel no more confident than they have ever felt of their ability to make decisions by themselves. A man who is ready enough to call himself an agnostic or even an atheist may show an interest in the influence of the stars, in spiritism, or in flipping a coin—things that are really a dead giveaway of his awareness of sources of power, knowledge, or control that are outside himself.

For the Christian there is a single source. It is God who is in charge of things, from stars to coins (though many would be slow to say that God has anything to do with heads or tails). It is reasonable for a Christian to go to God for help. Peter, a man not noted for steadfast faith, cried out, "Lord, save me!" when he found himself sinking in the sea. And the Lord immediately stretched out a hand to help.[1] It was an instant solution to the problem of the moment, which is exactly what we usually want.

This is a book about the guidance of God, but it is not six easy lessons on how to get it. It is a collection of observations from personal experience and from the Bible on why and how God does, in fact, guide his children.

Advice is a commodity we suddenly need and set out to get. We might spend a few dollars for a magazine, or a few dollars to have our tea leaves read, with the attitude, "Oh, well, it might work. What can I lose?" If we like what we hear, we can follow the advice. If not, we reject it. We might get the advice of friends without having to pay for it, and when we are in serious difficulty we may be willing to pay a great deal for professional advice. The higher the fee, the more concerned we will be to ascertain the qualifications of the source we are consulting. Is it trustworthy? But ours is still the choice—we can take it or leave it, according to our inclinations.

The Christian does not come to God for advice. He comes asking for God's will and, in the truest sense, there is no option here. Once it is known, it must be done. "Whoever knows what is right to do and fails to do it, for him it is sin."[2]

God's fee may be a higher one than we are prepared to pay—it may cost everything. Anybody who honestly intends to follow will certainly be asked to deny himself. A wealthy young man once came to Jesus full of good intentions, but they were short-lived. He went away sorrowful because Jesus had asked him to sell everything he owned.[3] That was too much.

To ask for the guidance of God is to make a choice, and this takes faith. It must be faith of a far higher kind than the breezy "If I like what I see I'll take it." It is the faith that has strength to wait for the rewards God holds, strength to believe they are worth waiting for, worth the price asked. Our prayers for guidance (or for anything else) really begin here: *I trust him.* This requires abandonment. We are no longer saying, "If I trust him, he'll give me such and such," but, "I trust him. Let him give me or withhold from me what he chooses."

Nothing I have to say here is new. It is a well-worn path that thousands have traveled; but I have written down in very simple terms
what I have seen on the way, hoping that one more witness will be an
encouragement to some who even in the 1990s believe there is a God
who can lighten our darkness.

1

the model prayer

Our Father, who art in heaven,
Hallowed be thy name.
Thy kingdom come.
Thy will be done on earth
    as it is in heaven.
Give us this day our daily bread,
And forgive us our trespasses
As we forgive those who trespass against us.
And lead us not into temptation,
But deliver us from evil,
For thine is the kingdom,
And the power, and the glory forever.
Amen.

A thoughtful consideration of the words of this prayer will help us to put our minds in the right frame before we begin knocking on God's door for guidance in some particular matter. This is the model prayer Jesus gave his disciples when they asked him to teach them to pray.

Twenty years have passed since I wrote the other chapters of this book; twenty years of seeking to be a more faithful follower of the Shepherd. He has been very patient with me, reviewing again and again lessons I should have learned half a century ago."How dull you are!" Jesus said to the two whom he met on the road to Emmaus. "How slow to believe!" (Luke 24:25 NEB). I am like those two. Coleridge said that many truths are commonly considered "so true as to lose all the powers of Truth, and lie bedridden in the dormitory of the soul."

The Lord's Prayer, I'm afraid, lay bedridden in the dormitory of my soul for a good many years. My father always ended his family prayer after breakfast with the words, "In the name of our Lord, Jesus Christ, who taught us to pray," whereupon all of us, down to the littlest who could speak, joined in saying the Lord's Prayer. Children memorize easily and we rattled it off without the least thought of the words, but my father understood the wisdom of teaching it (and hymns and Bible verses as well) long before we could appreciate the powers of the truths we parroted. The older I get, the more I see in that simple prayer and the more I use it (often many times a day), for I have come to see that it comprises all that really matters in life.

All? Yes, I really think it comprises all and therefore furnishes the context for all prayers, including, "Lead me, Lord. Show me what to do." Asking God to guide us is part of our daily prayers, but when we face what we call "big" decisions, we are more keenly aware of our need of a word from him. It is easy at such times to forget the pattern Jesus gave us. The urgent need of the moment obscures greater matters.

Many find that it helps to place our little prayers in the grand perspective of who God is and what his kingdom and his will require. Might it not be a good thing, before we launch into the subject of God's guidance, to do just that?

Our Father

When we address God we address the Creator of the Universe, the Ancient of Days, the Lord of Hosts, the Mighty God. The thought of him should inspire awe and reverence. But he is also the Everlasting *Father*. Jesus taught his disciples to call him *our* Father. If we trust the Son who died for us and come to the Father aware of our need of his grace, we may take our position before him as a child, not knowing what is best for us but coming and asking to be shown what to do. It is merely a request, not a demand, and can be granted or refused. Surely any father would look tenderly on a child's desire to be shown what to do. He will show him.

Our Father God *is* love, essential love, and therefore cannot possibly desire for his child anything but what is best.

He is all-wise and therefore knows just what that best is.

He is all-powerful and therefore can give what he wants to give.

His timing, his way of showing, and the thing shown may not be at all according to the child's expectation. But never mind. The Father will give all the help his child needs, will take him by the hand, and the child will learn.

Who Art in Heaven

The Father to whom we come is in *heaven*. We are on earth, where there are so many divergent pathways, such potential for choosing the wrong one. The mystery of prayer brings the finite into contact with the infinite, the temporal with the eternal, the seen with the unseen. This is a great comfort when we are asking to be shown what to do, for while we look at our own small world and the particular perplexity that brings us to the Father's knee, our minds fogged with doubts, anxieties, and frightening pictures of what the future may hold, he can see the end from the beginning. He is like the captain on the bridge who can see what the man in the engine room cannot. The far horizons, the positions of the stars, the direction of the wind are all known to the one who is in charge. Our heavenly Father knows every inch of our earthly journey, sees it whole, has been over the course himself, and says to us, "Fear thou not; for I am with thee: be not dismayed; for I am thy God: I will strengthen thee; yea, I will help thee; yea, I will uphold thee with the right hand of my righteousness" (Isa. 41:10).

Hallowed Be Thy Name

The modern mind can't make head or tail of this petition. Hallowed means holy. Isn't the name of God holy, perfectly holy, as holy as it can ever be? Why pray that it be hallowed? The answer may startle and humble us. God's love, longing for his children's participation with him by prayer, gives us a part to play in the hallowing (the making holy) of his name here on earth. The Father actually seeks worshipers, those who will worship him in spirit and in truth.

So this is an act of adoration. It is putting oneself at his feet, an essential preparation for all right action, a prayer that he may be glorified, remembering that we were created to be for "the praise of the glory of his grace" (Eph. 1:6). We finite creatures? Yes. All creatures were created for his glory: aardvarks, shrimps, great horned owls. But not all creatures pray—at least in the manner in which we men and women are meant to pray. By choosing to pray, we refer ourselves and all that concerns us—struggles, failures, hopes, dreams, relationships, work, perplexities, helplessnesses—to that holy name, the name that denotes the reality of God.

The next question is how? *How* shall we "hallow" his name? All the petitions that follow answer the question.

Thy Kingdom Come

Here we raise our sights far above our personal wants and ask for the realization of *his* kingdom, not our own. The matter for which we seek divine guidance we must now try to see in the light of God's *kingdom*, that stupendous realm of perfect order, goodness, light, love, peace, and joy. Down here on this fallen and broken planet, the planet we can't help but feel we have pretty well used up, it is hard to imagine God's kingdom coming, but we have been promised that it will, and for that coming we lift up our voice in prayer. We are telling our Father that that is what we want more than anything else. That is the real object of our prayer: *his* rule and reign and right ordering of all that is wrong.

As we put ourselves on his side, we hallow his name. As we lay our individual prayers before him, we do so recognizing that the answer has to fit into the coming of the kingdom and the holiness of the name, which means that the answer may be quite other than we suppose. The kingdom of God is the place where all is in perfect order, nothing is out of place, because it is the place where his will is always done. Therefore, when we ask for the coming of his kingdom, we are asking for the doing of his will.

Thy Will Be Done on Earth As It Is in Heaven

This is the point at which earth and heaven meet, the point at which my will must come into harmony with God's. Anything I am asking that is not in harmony with the way things are done in heaven has got to go. If in the integrity of my heart I speak the words, *Thy will be done*, I must be willing, if the answer requires it, that *my* will be undone. It is a prayer of commitment and relinquishment. The cost to Jesus of bringing his Father's kingdom on earth was the Cross of Calvary. Facing that cost, he sweated in Gethsemane: "O my Father, if it be possible . . ." (Matt. 26:39). Though his human flesh shrank at the prospect of death, he surrendered his own will to the will of the Father.

And thus he teaches us to pray for the coming of the kingdom in the only way the kingdom can possibly come: through the doing of the Father's will. There is no other way. This was Jesus' sole purpose in coming to earth. As we learn to live more intimately with him, it will become our sole object in life, and in every act that accords with his will, we are also hallowing his name.

He calls us not to passivity but to the dynamic self-abandonment that commitment to his kingdom means. This is the great prayer of the Church through the ages, *Thy will be done*, offered in company with the unseen throng of apostles, prophets, martyrs, and the Church throughout all the world.

To me it is a thrilling thing, when I stop to think about it, that when I pray for God's will to be done on earth as it is in heaven, I actually join, spiritually, that great company in heaven that ceaselessly prays about what is happening on earth. All of us are given the unspeakable privilege of offering ourselves as living sacrifices every time we repeat these words, *on earth*, that is, in me, in my house, my work, my life, *as it is in heaven*. When I try to picture the scene, I think of the words of Bishop Reginald Heber's hymn:

> The Son of God goes forth to war,
>   A kingly crown to gain;
> His blood-red banner streams afar;
>   Who follows in His train?
> Who best can drink His cup of woe
>   Triumphant over pain,
> Who patient bears His cross below—
>   He follows in His train.
>
> The martyr first, whose eagle eye
>   Could pierce beyond the grave,
> Who saw his Master in the sky,
>   And called on Him to save;
> Like Him, with pardon on His tongue,
>   In midst of mortal pain,
> He prayed for them that did the wrong:
>   Who follows in His train?
>
> A glorious band, the chosen few
>   On whom the Spirit came,
> Twelve valiant saints, their hope they knew,
>   And mocked the cross and flame;

They met the tyrant's brandished steel,
  The lion's gory mane;
They bowed their necks the death to feel,
  Who follows in their train?

A noble army, men and boys,
  The matron and the maid,
Around the Saviour's throne rejoice,
  In robes of light arrayed.
They climbed the steep ascent of heaven
  Through peril, toil, and pain:
O God, to us may grace be given
  To follow in their train.

Give Us This Day Our Daily Bread

With this petition we come down to the bottom of the stairs, as it were, down here where we live, the world of human needs and burdens and sins and limitations. The humble business of ordinary food and ordinary necessities reminds us of our utter dependence on God. We could not draw the next breath if it were not for his giving us life and breath. So we make our Declaration of Dependence in these simple words. When we look at them in contrast to the spiritual things prayed for first, they seem trivial. But the Lord *taught* us to pray this way. To him nothing is trivial or important, nothing small or great, for he is all and fills all in all. He will not have us imagining that material things are in themselves unworthy but are, in fact, his gifts and meant to be received gladly and humbly from his hand.

He made us human. He made us to need what he gives. He tells us to ask for it. Bread or something like it is the most basic human need. But I think we may include all human needs under this heading. Guidance is one of them.

I like to picture the Lord handing me a platter at the beginning of each new day. On it are the things he has chosen as best for me, and my prayer for daily bread is answered. My part is to *receive* whatever he gives. Guidance for a decision that need not be final until next Wednesday may require one small move or commitment today. I accept that and act on it without haggling with God because he has not yet granted me all the information I'm itching for. Perhaps *patience* is his gift of bread for today, or quietness, or the gift of uncertainty, that I may rest in his love, confident that when the time is ripe, the guidance will be clear.

Forgive Us Our Trespasses

This is my acknowledgment that I am not only human but sinful and in need of cleansing. Evelyn Underhill says our trespasses are our "voluntary share in the world's sinfulness." My shortcomings and excesses, debts and trespasses, my meanness and fear and envy, my selfishness of whatever sort—all these have their deleterious effect on those I love, those I live or work with, and on the world in general.

It seems that God must often delay the answer to our prayers for special guidance because we have already chosen a path of disobedience in that or some other matter. It is not reasonable to expect to be shown the right way when we deliberately continue in what we know is a wrong one. We must repent, which means to turn around. Go back to the point of departure. Then pray to be shown the path of God's will.

As We Forgive Those Who Trespass against Us

In these words, we agree to receive from God exactly the measure of forgiveness we mete out to those who have hurt us. If we hope for a clean slate from him, we must forgive from our *hearts* any who have wronged us, even if the wrong seems utterly unforgivable.

Have I been abused? Forgive me my trespasses in the same way I forgive the one who has abused me.

Have I been lied about? Forgive me as I have forgiven the liar.

Has someone cheated, abandoned, broken faith with, insulted, or violated me? Have I forgiven him from the depths of my heart? Lord, forgive me in the same measure.

If I cannot honestly say I have given the offender a perfectly clean slate, I must recognize the impossibility of God's forgiving me that which I insist upon retaining. Hatred and resentment are the very gates of hell. Because he is love, he will not, for very love, contribute to my self-destruction.

How shall I expect God to guide me if I refuse to follow his way? Only the merciful are promised mercy.

Lead Us Not into Temptation

This seems for some a puzzling prayer. Why would God lead us into temptation? We read in Exodus 13:17–18 (NIV) that he did not take Israel through the Philistine country after Pharaoh had let them go, though that would have been the shortest way. "If they face war," he said, "they might change their minds and return to Egypt." Here is a case where God knew the temptation would be too great for them to bear. He has promised never to allow us to be tempted beyond our powers of endurance (1 Cor. 10:13), and he wants us to side with him by praying.

Remember, once again, the Lord's Prayer was given to the apostles, that select band of godly men. They, even they, must remember their weakness. They must not seek heroics. The psalmist wrote, "Hold up my goings in thy paths, that my footsteps slip not" (Ps. 17:5).

Temptation is not in itself a sin. It is meant by "our ancient foe," Satan, to cause us to sin. God's purpose in allowing it is to test our faith, and his Word even tells us to *welcome* it, to count it *pure joy*, for that reason (James 1:2–3). We read that after Jesus was baptized, he was led *by the Spirit* into the wilderness for the express purpose of being tempted by the devil. Led to be tempted! But we are not to ask for that—again, no inflated ideas of our own heroic strength. We are weak and easily tempted to sin, so we ask the opposite. We pray for deliverance from temptation, for we might succumb.

Deliver Us from Evil

Uppermost in my mind when I pray this is that I may be purified of my own evil tendencies. Also I hope to be delivered from the evil of others. I cast myself completely on the Lord, trusting in the Absolute Love. He is my hope and my strength. I know no other ground.

Sometimes he hurts us. Hurt is not the same as harm. "There shall no evil befall thee, neither shall any plague come nigh thy dwelling" is an Old Testament promise (Ps. 91:10). Yet the Bible tells many stories of what is humanly called disaster striking God's own people. A careful reading of the biography of Joseph shows many terrible things happening to a good man, but the outcome reveals the care and love of a sovereign Lord throughout. Corrie ten Boom's godly father died in a concentration camp during Hitler's reign, and her sister starved to death, yet Corrie never doubted the love or the loving purpose of God. They were not delivered from the evil of the Nazis, but they were *kept*—kept in God's arms, kept in peace. No harm, in the eternal sense, ever touched them. In his time the pattern of his working will be unfolded. We can pray with perfect confidence, "Deliver us from evil," knowing that he may hurt us, but he will never harm us.

"Though I walk in the midst of trouble, thou wilt revive me: thou shalt stretch forth thine hand against the wrath of mine enemies, and thy right hand shall save me. The LORD will perfect that which concerneth me: thy mercy, O LORD, endureth for ever" (Ps. 138:7–8).

> He leadeth me in the paths of righteousness
> for his name's sake.
>
> Psalm 23:3

2

what is promised

Two young Americans with high adventure in their hearts arrived in the city of Quito, Ecuador, on their way to the "Great Amazon Rain Forest" east of the Andes. They were going on a six-week trek and planned to write a book about their experiences. (Six weeks ought to be enough for that, oughtn't it?) They had been to an army surplus store before they left home and bought everything the salesman told them they would need—things like waterproof hammocks with built-in mosquito nets, canvas water bags, insect repellent, snakebite kits, machetes, pith helmets, fancy pocket knives, pressure lanterns, floating flashlights, safari shirts and shorts, guns and ammunition, fish hooks, reels, rods, bait and sinkers, dehydrated foods, cooking utensils, and heavy leather combat boots with extra high tops to prevent snakebite. What more could they want? There was, it occurred to them when they reached Quito, one thing—the language—and when they learned that a jungle missionary was in town, they came to see me.

There would be Indians where they were going, wouldn't there? Well, maybe, but that would depend on exactly where. Quichuas? That, too, would depend. There were seven or eight tribes in that side of the Andes. The men were a little vague about the route they would take, but it looked as if they were going where they would not find any inhabitants at all, or, if they did, they would not be Quichuas.

"Oh, well, just give us a few phrases," they said. "Indian languages are pretty much the same anyway, aren't they?"

They described their equipment to me with great pride, and I could see that it was not going to be of much use. I wanted to tell them that what they ought to have was a guide, but they had asked only for help on the language and not for advice. So off they went, full of confidence. Perhaps they found their way all right, survived, and even wrote the book. I never heard of them again.

Sometimes we come to God as the two adventurers came to me—confident and, we think, well-informed and well-equipped. But it has occurred to us that with all our accumulation of stuff, something is missing. There is just one thing we will have to ask God for, and we hope he will not find it necessary to sort through the other things. There's nothing there that we're willing to do without. We know what we need—a yes or no answer, please, to a simple question. Or perhaps a road sign. Something quick and easy to point the way.

What we really ought to have is the Guide himself. Maps, road signs, a few useful phrases are good things, but infinitely better is someone who has been there before and knows the way.

Is there someone?

The Lord is my Shepherd.[1] He can see to everything if we are willing to turn it all over (even the equipment, even the route), but we will not do this unless we believe he means what he says. Can his word be trusted? He has made countless promises. Is he going to fulfill them?

To say yes to these questions is to have faith. It is to start following. The sheep, trusting the shepherd, trots after him down the trail.

But the picture of the Eastern shepherd with his robes and staff, the flock of sheep, the stony path through the ravine, the dark valley, and the grassy place with the quiet pool are so remote from our lives as to seem no more than a romantic painting from another country and another age. We live in towns and cities and suburbs. Our days are full of perplexities far removed from the things that bother rams and ewes and lambs. We muddle along through the thousand decisions of an ordinary day. When we are aware of the need for help in one of them, it is not one relating to good pasturage or a water supply. Time and money fill our minds: how to get them, how to use them, how to save them. Where shall I set the thermostat today? The price of fuel has gone up so frighteningly. And for breakfast—have I time to make pancakes? Can we afford bacon? Should the children take their lunches to school (it takes time to make a lunch) or should they buy them (it costs two dollars)? Shall I take the freeway to work today and pay a bridge toll, or shall I save the money and spend the time to go the long way? Silly things, trivialities, but we cannot escape them.

Then there are the serious things. A student has to decide where to go to college, what to major in, whom to marry, what job to prepare for, where to find that job. After college he must decide where to live, how to pay for the house, the car, the furniture, the things that seem so much more indispensable than green pastures.

But the God of the pastures is, let us not forget, the God of everywhere else. He knows just as much about suburbia or the inner city. He is not at a loss to know what to do with us, no matter where we are or what we are anxious about. Every last thing that enters our heads is known to him.

But the "guidance of God"—is it reasonable to expect such a thing in this day and age? Has he ever made any promises that I can get hold of? Is there anything that applies to my needs this Tuesday? Are the promises (to use a badly overworked word) *relevant*? Might not the advice of a trained guidance expert be more likely to help me?

When the question of relevancy is raised, the next question ought to be: relevant to what? As C. S. Lewis said, "All that is not eternal is eternally out of date."[2] The Bible is relevant—more relevant, I am convinced, more accurate, more trustworthy, more totally applicable to my "case" as a human being than anything a man, no matter how well-trained, can tell me. It is the place to begin. It is the foundation, the only sure one. What I learn from other sources may help me a great deal, as stones to be laid on the foundation, and it would be foolish of me to brush aside other kinds of help that might be available to me. They are good gifts, and gifts of whatever kind come to us, we are told, from the Father of lights.[3] But we can start with the Bible.

We are talking about guidance of the most fundamental kind. Although the shepherd picture may, at a superficial glance, look irrelevant to modern life, a deeper understanding of what is taught in that beautiful Twenty-third Psalm may come to us when we find ourselves in a crisis. If we actually experience the valley of the shadow, everything but the Living Word of God may then look utterly irrelevant. A man learns he has an incurable disease. A house burns to the ground, destroying a manuscript on which years have been spent. A business fails. A son or daughter rejects the way his parents have taught him and breaks their hearts. Death comes into our house.

The question of relevancy at such a time is turned completely over. The news on television, the menu for dinner, the committee meeting—all that occupied our days suddenly becomes meaningless. The familiar looks unfamiliar (who has not felt the incongruity of the sun's shining as usual when our world has collapsed?), and we lose our bearings. Rock walls on all sides, shadows, no escape—and all at once the words shine like a light. "Yea, though I walk through the valley of the shadow of death, I will fear no evil: for thou art with me."[4] Perhaps then, for the first time, we know ourselves to be sheep—stupid, helpless, bewildered, and desperate. We need not then rush out and search frantically for a shepherd. He's there. He is our Shepherd. He hasn't, for a single moment, forgotten his job.

I suppose it was because my mother so often had to say to us children, "How many times have I told you?" that I was impressed, when a very small child, with the words of the hymn "How Firm a Foundation": "What more can He say than to you He hath said?" God had to repeat things, too. He had said all we needed to hear, and yet we had not heard. Had he to say them over and over to us? Yes. That was the truth of it. The Bible contains thousands of promises, a great number of which concern guidance. Nearly every one of the sixty-six books has some word about how God led someone or how he promises to lead those who want to be led, from the Lord God's taking the man Adam and putting him in the garden he had made for him, telling him what to do and what not to do, to the Lamb's leading those who have washed their robes: "And he will guide them to springs of living water; and God will wipe away every tear from their eyes."[5]

There are promises of special care for special needs: "He will feed his flock like a shepherd, he will gather the lambs in his arms, he will carry them in his bosom, and gently lead those that are with young."[6]

If you can't see the way before you: "I will lead the blind in a way that they know not, in paths that they have not known I will guide them. I will turn the darkness before them into light, the rough places into level ground."[7]

If you are thirsty or in need of refreshment of some kind: "He who has pity on them will lead them, and by springs of water will guide them."[8]

If no way looks possible at all: "And I will make my mountains a way, and my highways shall be raised up."[9]

If you are confused or distressed: "I will lead him and requite him with comfort."[10]

If you falter or are fearing failure: "Thou hast delivered my soul from death: wilt not thou deliver my feet from falling . . . ?"[11]

If you are lonely or tired: "My presence shall go with thee, and I will give thee rest."[12]

Is this what you would call a relevant list? Does it touch on anything you need right now? They are all promises dependent on the presence of the Guide himself.

I would far rather have a guide than the best advice or the clearest set of directions.

When I lived in the forest of Ecuador, I usually traveled on foot. Except for one occasion when I went off alone (and quickly learned what a bad mistake that was), I always had with me a guide who knew the way or knew much better than I did how to find it. Trails often led through streams and rivers that we had to wade, but sometimes there was a log laid high above the water we had to cross.

I dreaded those logs and was always tempted to take the steep, hard way down into the ravine and up the other side. But the Indians would say, "Just walk across, señorita," and over they would go, confident and light-footed. I was barefoot as they were, but it was not enough. On the log, I couldn't keep from looking down at the river below. I knew I would slip. I had never been any good at balancing myself on the tops of walls and things, and the log looked impossible. So my guide would stretch out a hand, and the touch of it was all I needed. I stopped worrying about slipping. I stopped looking down at the river or even at the log and looked at the guide, who held my hand with only the lightest touch. When I reached the other side, I realized that if I had slipped he could not have held me. But his being there and his touch were all I needed.

The analogy breaks down, of course. If our Guide is God, he can hold us from any slipping. He could, if he chose, carry us across bodily. But the lesson the Indians taught me was that of trust. The only thing I really needed, the touch of a steady hand, they could provide. If I had been inclined to come to a halt in the middle of the log and raise nasty questions or argue their ability to keep me from falling, my trust would have collapsed and so would I.

I have found in the Bible plenty of evidence that God has guided people. I find, too, assurance that he is willing to guide me. He has been at it for a long time. His hand reaches toward me. I have only to take it.

3

the conditions

We have ample evidence that the Lord is able to guide. The promises cover every imaginable situation. All we need to do is to take the hand he stretches out. But it is here that the hardest question arises for me. How, exactly, do I take his hand? Isn't this an extreme oversimplification of the conditions of the promises?

I know he has said over and over, "I will guide you." I know the words, "It is the Lord who goes before you; he will be with you, he will not fail you or forsake you; do not fear or be dismayed."[1] But there are so many promises with conditions attached, conditions that seem impossible to fulfill for us who are not far along the road to sainthood. Often I have prayed to God for light, and he has shown me some promise in the Bible that indicates he will certainly give me the light I am asking for, *if*—and then I have found, to my despair, that a great deal is asked of me in exchange. Who does God think I am, that I can meet such demands before he will answer my prayer?

The Recognition of Who God Is

The first condition is the recognition of God himself. It is not who does he think I am, but who do I think he is. I confess that after many years I am still having to go back often to this, to Lesson 1 in the school of faith. I forget what I learned. I started out on false premises: who I am, what I need, why my case is special, what I'm hoping for, what I pray for, or something—anything but the thing that matters most: who God is.

To learn who he is, we go to the Bible. The Bible is a Book about God. It tells us all we need to know about him, and it shows us how he makes himself known to human beings. The Old Testament begins with God's relation to one man, Adam, and takes us through the story of how he led the people of Israel, a race he had chosen to bear his name. The words "lead" and "guide" occur much more often in the Old Testament than in the New. God's guidance of Israel was literal and specific, and most of us find it easier to understand than his dealings with people in the New Testament. The rules were laid down quite clearly (written out, in fact, on stone tablets to begin with), the journey was from Point A to Point B to Point C, the pillars of cloud and fire were easy to see.

Then, too, the Israelites were a group. God led them like a flock. They all took the same route, suffered the same privations, witnessed the same miracles. But if we read carefully, we see that God never lumped them together in a single faceless mass. The responses of individuals varied. Some rejected the Word of God and "left their bones in the desert."[2] Some simply refused to trust.

The New Testament is another story. The first four books, called the Gospels, give us the life of Jesus. This was a human life, lived on earth to show us, in a way we can comprehend, what God is like. The God of the Old Testament, who called himself the God of Abraham, Isaac, and Jacob, is the same God who showed himself in the New Testament in the Person of Jesus Christ. "Anyone who has seen me," Jesus said, "has seen the Father."[3] A man's response to Jesus is his response to God.

The people of Israel had no Scriptures in their hands. The people in the time of Christ had only the Old Testament. Today we have both the Old and New Testaments, the latter interpreting the former.

When we speak of the recognition of who God is, we need to take into account all that he has revealed about himself in the whole Bible. But not all at once. That would be too much for any of us. We can only come as we are, with a readiness to be shown. "Whoever would draw near to God must believe that he exists and that he rewards those who seek him."[4] This is what Abraham did, and he was called a man of faith. We can be Abraham's children by faith. This makes us a part of the group, sheep in the flock called the Church in the New Testament, eligible for the Shepherd's guidance.

When asking God for guidance in some individual matter, it is a good thing to have as a background some inkling of the larger picture so we see our own position in that perspective.

I love to study the biographies of the Bible as biographies, to learn what sort of event in a man's life the Spirit of God regarded as worth mentioning. I find not just one but many instances of God's going to great lengths in order to get a man's attention long enough to say to him "I am." And in most instances, the man had to be isolated in some way.

Abraham had to leave behind all that was familiar to him, and it was then, in a strange country, that God said, "Fear not . . . I am your shield."[5]

Jacob, away from home in Bethel, asleep with his head on a rock, saw the Lord in a dream saying, "I am the LORD . . . I am with you . . . I will not leave you."[6]

Moses, tending a flock in the wilderness, heard the voice of God from the awesome burning bush: "I am the God of your father . . . I have seen . . . have heard . . . I know . . . I have come down to deliver . . . I will be with you."[7]

King Nebuchadnezzar was stripped of his power and made to live like an animal until he recognized who God was.[8]

The apostle Paul, when he was still called Saul, zealous persecutor of Christians, was stopped in his tracks and confronted with that terrible revelation, "I am Jesus."[9] After Jesus had identified himself, he gave the order Paul was to carry out.

When John was in exile on the island of Patmos, probably an old and very lonely man, he was given the vision of one like a son of man who said, "Fear not, I *am* the first and the last . . . I died . . . I am alive . . . I have the keys." Then came the order: "Now write what you see."[10] First the *I am*. Then the *do this*.

Pharaoh, refusing to recognize who God was, had the audacity to disobey. "Who is the LORD," he said to Moses and Aaron, "that I should heed his voice and let Israel go? I do not know the LORD, and moreover I will not let Israel go."[11]

If we want to know what to do, we need to know first who will tell us.

"Be still, and know that I am God."[12]

If we have once shut up long enough to know this, we have, at least in that moment, been ready to obey. But it is the being still that is so hard for us. It often takes illness, loss, suffering of some kind, isolation, and loneliness. Only when we have come to the end of our own resources, when few distractions are left to us, does it become possible to be quiet.

But if, in the providence of God, we have not yet had to weather a real crisis, we may "be still" on purpose. We may choose to obey the command, stop all activity, turn aside in stillness, and know. The best kind of beginning, when we are wanting to know the will of God, is to concentrate first on God himself. And of course, the briefest effort to do this will humble us, for we will learn how poorly we are in control of our thoughts. For me, there is nothing like the printed word to help me corral my scattered thoughts. Simply looking at a verse in the Bible that tells me something of God and reading through a hymn or a prayer are aids to discipline, and I need all the aids I can get.

I have been told that in one of the China Inland Mission homes in China there was a motto on the wall that said, "The sun stood still. The iron did swim. This God is our God for ever and ever. He will be our guide even unto death." This God, the One who, in answer to the prayer of an ordinary man, stopped the sun in its course, the God who suspended his own law of gravity and made an ax head float, this is the

God to whom I come.[13] This is the God whose will and direction I am asking. This God is the One whose promises I am counting on. And can he help me out of my predicament? Whatever my predicament may be, as soon as I compare it with the circumstances surrounding the miracles of the sun and the ax, my doubts seem comical.

God knows all about those comical doubts. He knows our frame. He remembers that we are dust, and it is to us, knowing all this better than we know it ourselves, that he made those promises.

God is, according to Isaiah 43, our Creator, our Redeemer, the Lord our God, the Holy One of Israel, our Savior. Would we ask him to be anything more than this, before we admit in our hearts that he can be trusted? He is called also El Shaddai, "the God who is Enough."[14] Will we settle for that?

I have called this—the recognition of who God is—the first condition. Perhaps it would be better to call it the primary condition, for it is not one we can fulfill once and for all and then move beyond. The recognition of who God is is a lifetime process. Nor does it end with our earthly life. "This is eternal life, that they know thee the only true God, and Jesus Christ whom thou hast sent."[15] The process of knowing him modifies the quality of our lives. It is a continual fulfillment and a continual attraction. "Let us know," the prophet Hosea wrote; "let us press on to know the LORD; his going forth is sure as the dawn; he will come to us as the showers, as the spring rains that water the earth."[16]

The quality of our lives is transformed not only by our initial response to Christ but also by the daily answer of faith to whatever a day holds. If we have, perhaps through some small incident, come to a new knowledge of our own sin, we then recognize him as Savior. In our sorrow we learn that he is the Comforter. In perplexity he shows himself as our Counselor. Our weakness gives us occasion to call on him as the Mighty God, Strength, Fortress, Deliverer, and Refuge.

The prophet Habakkuk saw the God of Israel not as a tender Shepherd but as a raging Giant: "Thou didst bestride the earth in fury, thou didst trample the nations in anger. Thou wentest forth for the salvation of thy people, for the salvation of thy anointed. Thou didst crush the head of the wicked, laying him bare from thigh to neck. . . . Thou didst trample the sea with thy horses." This representation of power is followed by Habakkuk's testimony of faith: "God, the Lord, is my strength; he makes my feet like hinds' feet, he makes me tread upon my high places."[17] That fearful deity, that Giant who roars forth for the deliverance of his people, is the God who makes us able to walk where it seems there can be no walking.

Although the first condition, as a lifetime and even an eternal process, may overwhelm us, we will find, if we are willing to look, that whatever happens today affords ample opportunity to make a beginning. The Gospels can help us see how this works. They are full of stories of how Jesus met individual men and women, in the ordinary course of their lives, and did things for them.

One example is the story in Mark 9 of the man who brought his son, who was possessed by a "dumb spirit." After describing the torment the boy had suffered, the father said, "If you can do anything, have pity on us and help us."

There is not much faith in those words. But Jesus said, "If you can! All things are possible to him who believes."

"I believe!" cried the father. "Help my unbelief."[18]

He had, like most of us, only the faintest recognition of Jesus—a good Man, he had heard, one who did some wonderful things and taught well. So with the feeblest hope (but it was hope) he had come. He *had* come, and he had brought with him his suffering child. He had, in that act, fulfilled the first condition. He had come to the right Man, the only One who could do what needed to be done. The issue now rested not on "If you can do anything" but, as Jesus told him, "If you can believe." So the man believed.

Belief

Belief is the second condition, clearly dependent upon the first. We are asked to have faith. Faith means, for one thing, believing that

God means what he says. If we have really recognized him, we will be able to trust his word. Jesus told the epileptic boy's father in Mark's story that all things are possible to the one who believes. The father had been hoping for an impossible thing. ("Faith is the assurance of things hoped for, the conviction of things not seen."[19]) In a flash he responded, "I believe!" Here, as in other Gospel stories, the act of coming was followed by the verbal declaration of belief. Even then the demon did not vanish automatically. There followed Jesus' word of command, then noise and convulsions, then minutes that were an eternity of stunned silence when the child appeared to be dead. The father had time, I think, to wish with all his soul he could take back those rash words "I believe." They must have seemed for a few seconds the words of a madman. At last Jesus took the boy's hand, and the boy got up. In that short space of time, the father went from the flimsiest kind of faith to terror-stricken doubt to the place where faith became sight. The story is a short version of the life of faith, for it shows us quickly, and in a form we can take in, where it all starts.

The Obedience of Faith

The recognition of who God is and faith in him—are these two conditions enough? What of all those stringent conditions such as:

"He is in the way of life that *keepeth instruction*."[20]
"The steps of a *good man* are ordered by the LORD."[21]
"The *meek* will he guide in judgment."[22]
"The integrity of the *upright* guides them."[23]
"He who does these things [walks blamelessly, and does what is right, and speaks truth from his heart; who does not slander with his tongue, and does no evil to his friend, and six more things] shall never be moved."[24]
"*If* you take away from the midst of you the yoke, the pointing of the finger, and speaking wickedness, *if* you pour yourself out for

the hungry and satisfy the desire of the afflicted, *then* shall your
light rise in the darkness and your gloom be as the noonday."[25]

The list could be much longer. The Old Testament reiterates what
is expected of the godly man. In his earliest dealings with the people
of Israel, God asked obedience and they disobeyed. God gave them
promises, dependent on their willingness to do what he asked, and
they did not do it. But he did not give them up. It was the glory
of his own name that was at stake. If in fact he was their Creator,
Redeemer, and Savior, if he had chosen them as a people to bear his
name and had entered into a covenant relationship with them, he
must take the responsibility of that glory upon himself. In countless
ways he bore with them, corrected them, punished them, goaded
them, and brought them to the promised land. His love for them
was inexorable.

Israel's travels in the Old Testament graphically illustrate what
it means to be guided by God. In the New Testament, to become a
follower is called discipleship. The conditions for this look humanly
unattainable:

If any man would come after me, let him deny himself and take up
his cross and follow me. For whoever would save his life will lose it,
and whoever loses his life for my sake will find it.[26]

No one can serve two masters.[27]

He who loves father or mother more than me is not worthy of me; and
he who loves son or daughter more than me is not worthy of me; and
he who does not take his cross and follow me is not worthy of me.[28]

At this point I want to cry, *Stop!* Don't tell me any more. I can't
fulfill the conditions. I do not "keep instruction." I hardly listen to it,
in fact. I am not "godly." I am not good or meek or upright or blameless
or truthful or self-sacrificing in any sense at all except a relative one
(surely I am no worse than most?). Even a casual look at God's Word

shows me that a relative goodness won't do. I am none of the things I am told I need to be in order to expect God's guidance. The thing I needed so desperately and wanted to pray for so simply looks now like a carrot on a stick. It is no simple thing that I can reach a hand to take. The illustration of the Indian on the log only mocks me. I must attain some point of perfection before I can even begin to ask, so I can't qualify, now or ever.

The consciousness of my own imperfection implies a consciousness of perfection. Intuitively we know that if there is such a thing as a relative goodness there is such a thing as absolute goodness, and before that goodness we shrink and are afraid. There is nowhere to turn. Like C. S. Lewis, as he described his own conversion, with eyes darting right and left in search of some escape, we find that there is none.[29] There is nowhere to turn but back to him whom we dread.

Graham Greene tells us in his autobiography that he came "to the limit of the land and there the sea waited, if I didn't turn back. I was laughing to keep my courage up."[30] Thomas Binney has expressed it in his hymn, "Eternal Light":

> Oh how shall I, whose native sphere
>   Is dark, whose mind is dim,
> Before the Ineffable appear
> And on my naked spirit bear
>   The uncreated beam?

How shall we? We can retreat into darkness, refusing the way of escape and shutting ourselves off from rescue. But Binney goes on to answer the question:

> There is a way for man to rise
>   To that sublime abode;
> An offering and a sacrifice,
> A Holy Spirit's energies,
>   An Advocate with God.

So all those other conditions that look like insurmountable barriers to our ever getting the light we are looking for become, in and of themselves, matters of faith. We cannot do them by ourselves, so we trust God to do them for us.

We are back to the analogy of the guide and the log across the ravine. The truth is that the whole thing has been done for us—Jesus is our Guide, and he is himself the Way. My sins are those ravines, the gaps I cannot cross by myself, the interruptions along the way. But there is a way across. Logs have been laid and Someone is there to help me walk on them. However, we don't need to cross all of the logs at once. We take them as they come, and it is the same Guide who helps us over each one. We go with him.

The Glory of the Name

In Africa during the earlier part of this century, men called "white hunters" built up for themselves a good reputation as guides. They knew where the animals were and they charged high prices to lead foreign hunters to where they could shoot them. It was not only the big game the foreigners paid for but the big name of the guide as well. A high reputation carries a high responsibility.

Old Testament writers made much of the name of God. Israel was a nation specifically set apart as a place for God to put his name. Appeals were made on the basis of the name. "For thy name's sake lead me, and guide me,"[31] the psalmist prayed. Not because of who I am, not in recognition of my reputation, but because of who you are. "And his name will be called 'Wonderful Counselor.'" "The LORD is my banner." "LORD God of Hosts."[32] No questions of merit can arise with regard to that name. It is above every name. Therefore I can come today on the ground of that name's merit.

The prayer that Jesus taught his disciples begins with the petition, "Our Father who art in heaven, Hallowed be thy name."[33] Whatever our requests may be that bring us to his feet, they should begin with a careful consideration of the meaning of this form of address. If we

41

say the words slowly and thoughtfully, they cannot help but color the rest of the prayer. If it is guidance we are asking, we may be very wrong in our hopes as to the direction it will take. We may be ill-prepared in heart for the road God will choose for us. But, as George MacDonald wrote, "The thought of him to whom that prayer goes will purify and correct the desire."[34]

If we did not have God's unequivocal promise, the words "Guide *me*, for the sake of *your* name" would sound outrageously presumptuous. But the truth is that God said he would do just this. There is nothing presumptuous or precarious about it. The validity of the divine word is at stake, and that is a very sure foundation.

Making a Beginning

Before a man begins building he must make sure of the foundation. Hearing and doing the Word—this is the bedrock of faith. Jesus made this simple enough for children to understand in his story of the two men who built houses, one on rock, one on sand.[35] We all know what happened in the storm. The stability of one house is the picture of the man who hears the Word of God and does it. For me, it is wonderfully reassuring to know that this does not mean knowing all the Word, being perfectly obedient to all the Word, at one time. Hearing one thing, doing that one thing, is what is required. This puts me in touch with God, which is precisely what we mean when we speak of an "act of faith." "It is only when we obey God's laws that we can be quite sure that we really know him," John wrote.[36]

When a child begins to walk, his first step is reason enough, in his parents' eyes, for enthusiastic praise. The step is not a very successful one. It is wobbly and may take the child where he didn't mean to go faster than he wanted. But it contains the elements of walking—putting one foot in front of the other. Doing this over and over will eventually get the child somewhere.

To believe one thing—this one promise that God will guide us, for example—is a baby step. It is a beginning of a walk with God. The steps that follow will be like the first one in that they contain the element of faith. If God means it this time, he means it the next time. I take him at his word now, and I will hear another word tomorrow.

For the baby, walking soon becomes easy. I do not think this is quite analogous to our walk with God. There is a sense, of course, in which seeing a promise fulfilled gives us confidence. But it is also true that each step of faith is a step of *faith*, and there is always the void beneath, the dark ravine. Jesus, called the "pioneer and perfecter of our faith," had to learn obedience,[37] and the lessons during his life on earth certainly did not get easier. On the night before his crucifixion he sweated over the will of his Father. He was, as J. B. Phillips translates it, "horror-stricken and desperately depressed." But he was still able to say, "O my Father!"[38]

For us, the road may have varying degrees of difficulty. But the Pioneer has traveled it before us. There will be no ravines he cannot cross. He knows the way; he has been over every foot of it. "This God is our God. . . . He will be our guide."[39]

Prayer and Fasting

We ought to pray for guidance. Paul's letters contain many prayers for Christians, that they might know and do the will of God. A strong recognition of who God is, a strong affirmation of faith in him, runs through those letters. "I know whom I have believed,"[40] Paul wrote to the young man Timothy in a letter meant to give him courage in his life of faith. Paul himself had started out on what he thought was service to God, but after years of fervent activity he had experienced the shock of recognition on the road to Damascus—recognition that, far from serving the Lord, he had been persecuting him. This produced a total change in Paul's life. He had a new knowledge, a new belief, and a new kind of activity.

Faith requires action. Perhaps the most "natural" activity is prayer. If we know the one in whom we have believed, we turn to him for help. I have not compiled statistics, but it seems to me that the single kind of help most frequently prayed for in the Bible is guidance. In the Psalms alone we find these:[41]

> "Lead me ... in thy righteousness."
> "Lead me in thy truth."
> "Lead me on a level path."
> "For thy name's sake lead me, and guide me."
> "Send out thy light and thy truth: let them lead me."
> "Lead thou me to the rock that is higher than I."
> "Search me, O God, and know my heart ... and lead me in the way everlasting."
> "Let thy good spirit lead me on a level path!"

It is possible that we may say to ourselves, "If God has promised to lead me, what is the point of my always asking him to?" But the examples of Scripture show us that godly men who knew those promises very well prayed continually. The simple bringing of the request to God is an acknowledgment, both to ourselves and to him, that we need him. It is an act of faith in itself, a stretching out of our hands to our Guide, hence a good way to prepare ourselves for whatever his leading may be.

When Jesus taught his disciples to pray, he did not explain all the mysteries we glimpse there. He simply told them what to say. "Thy will be done" and "Lead us not into temptation" concern specifically the matter we are discussing. The fact that the short prayer Jesus gave the disciples includes the matter of guidance assures us it is an entirely proper request.

But why, instead of praying positively as the psalmist did, "Lead me in thy righteousness," did Jesus tell us to ask "Lead us not into temptation"?

Is it likely that the Lord who is our Shepherd, who loves us even to death, would lead us into temptation? It is a strange request, and one great minds have wrestled with. Perhaps a partial explanation is that here the one who prays takes it for granted he is being led, as though he had said, "I'm right behind you, Lord, I'm following, go on leading me. But not—please, Lord, *not* into temptation. I am weak." The New English Bible translates it, "Do not put us to the test." It is a very human prayer (it mentions food before it mentions temptation), and as such shows us how thorough was Jesus' understanding of our human limitations and tears. We dread tests or examinations of any sort. If there's anything we would rather not know it's what is wrong with us. We know too many things without being shown more. Don't turn on any bright lights. Deliver us from evil. We can't avoid it ourselves. Show us the way out. We're following.

Not many of us come to God for the first time with the intention of putting ourselves into his hands for the rest of our lives. We haven't thought that far. We need guidance in one particular matter, and usually we have already exhausted other sources without success. There is nothing left to do now but pray about it, and we make an emergency call: "Help, please!"

Many people in the Gospel accounts met Jesus in this way. They heard he was passing by and rushed out to get help. He did not rebuke them for this opportunism. He stopped and confronted them, sometimes requiring that they state exactly what it was they wanted, even when it must have been obvious to everyone around. Imagine a famous healer asking a blind man, "What is it you want?" The statement of the need was a necessary condition for his meeting it. But how many of them understood that there was far more for them than they had dreamed of asking? How many saw the possibilities beyond the healed hand, the loaves and fishes, or the tubs of wine at a party? If only the Samaritan woman had recognized him she would have asked for the Water of Life. Not even the disciples themselves grasped very much of what was offered to them, but the love and grace of Jesus kept pouring out.

Prayer is the statement of a need. "Let your requests be made known unto God."[42] Doesn't he know about them? He does, but that is not the point. We need to come to his feet. "Tell God every detail of your needs in thankful prayer."[43]

Sometimes, to make sure I don't forget the details, I make a list. The necessity of recalling all the things that have any bearing on my need for guidance—the pros and cons of all the possible courses that seem open, the circumstances which look to me significant, the reasons I have for wanting one thing above another—helps me to sort out exactly what it is I am asking. And sometimes, through this sorting, I see that I ought to ask something quite different. So Paul's advice to tell God the details may actually contain the solution. The fact that I am telling God, too, makes them look different. It casts a different light. "In thy light shall we see light."[44] All my muddle-headed thinking before I started praying was a waste of time and only kept me in the dark.

When I was young I had the idea (I am sure I must have heard sermons on this) that I would somehow have to annihilate my own will before I could properly pray to God for his. "You must have absolutely no will of your own in the matter," someone had said. This sounded all right to me, and I spent a lot of time and energy trying to follow this advice. Finally I saw that no such thing was required. The struggle Jesus had in the Garden of Gethsemane showed me this. A conflict was taking place—not to annihilate his own will but to accept the will of the Father, which was *other* than his. It did not end with Jesus saying, "My will is now thine" but with, "Not my will but thine be done." The act of praying, far from divesting us of human desires, enables us to lay them before God as very real and pressing and say to him, "Not these, Lord. Yours." (If we had gotten rid of them, there would be nothing to lay down.)

There is something terribly down-to-earth about this. They are my own requests I am supposed to "make known" to God. They are things I feel strongly about. They may be sinful. If they are, making them known to God might make plain to me their true nature. But I start by making them known. I pray for what I want, as a child asks its father for whatever it wants. This is faith's legitimate activity.

Sometimes a father's answer to his child is no. If God, like a father, denies us what we want now, it is in order to give us some far better thing later on. The will of God, we can rest assured, is invariably a better thing, but our having asked for what we wanted now provides the occasion for us to say, "Nevertheless not my will but thine be done."

In praying for guidance, I find I usually have some solution in mind that looks attractive to me. I want God to guide me, but I am hoping it will be in my way. What my prayer amounts to is approval of my plan. I know this and God knows it and there is no use pretending it isn't so. Paul found himself in terrific conflicts of interest. He wrote:

> My own behaviour baffles me. For I find myself doing what I really loathe but not doing what I really want to do. Yet surely if I do things that I really don't want to do, I am admitting that I really agree that the Law is good. But it cannot be said that "I" am doing them at all—it must be sin that has made its home in my nature. And, indeed, I know from experience that the carnal side of my being can scarcely be called the home of good! I often find that I have the will to do good, but not the power. That is, I don't accomplish the good I set out to do, and the evil I don't really want to do I find I am always doing.[45]

This is the story of our lives. And the only way out is the way Paul goes on to describe: the new life in Christ, which is strictly a matter of faith.[46]

I am by nature so skeptical that I am nearly always doubting my own (not to speak of others') sincerity, so that when I pray for God's will in a matter it is no easy thing to convince myself that I really want it.

One way of taking myself in hand is fasting. I have not done this often, but at times when the most difficult decisions faced me I have found it helpful. It seems to me a sensible way of proving (again, as in the bringing of requests to God, it is proof to myself and to him) that I am serious. I like to eat, and fasting is not a good way of getting one's mind off food, but it is a way of deliberately putting one's mind on one thing (God) because you are reminded every minute of the other thing (food). The fact that you have made up your mind not to eat keeps before you the reason you are not eating. You are after something specific from God, and although your own will may be too weak to will his will, it is at least strong enough for this one small thing. God in his mercy and fatherly love takes note of this flicker of movement toward him. He sees the heart and he sees if we, like Daniel, have purposed in our hearts regarding the matter of eating—for once purposed seriously enough, that is, to do something about it. God has met me on such occasions, and his kindness in response to so simple an act, an act available to anybody anytime, cheered me.

One Man's Cross

"If any man would come after me, let him deny himself and take up his cross daily and follow me."[47] Jesus' words imply that there is a cross that is meant for each individual. It is peculiar to him, something that no one else could take up for him even if he wanted to. The taking up of that cross must be an act of the will, a thing one might refuse to do. But it is the prerequisite if he is serious about following.

Things that are not at all matters of choice are often called "crosses." Blindness, deafness, or some other physical disability, a retarded child or a disobedient and ungrateful child, a drunken husband, senile parents to care for, poverty or loss or limitation of any kind are all things about which people sometimes say, "Well, I guess that's the cross I'm supposed to bear." But of course such things are required of any human being regardless of whether he has any intention of following Christ. In some of them there may be room for a certain amount of choice, but unless the choice is made for the sake of Christ rather than for some other reason (for example, saving face: "What would people think if I didn't do this?"), it has little to do with the taking up of the cross Christ was speaking of.

What is that cross? It is, I believe, the thing required of me today. "Let him take up his cross *daily*," Jesus said, "and follow me." Some duty lies on my doorstep right now. It may be a simple thing I have known for a long time I ought to do, but it has been easy to avoid. It is probably the thing that springs to my mind when I pray the prayer, "We have left undone those things which we ought to have done."[48]

It may be that, although I have been doing something I ought to do, I have never done it without grudging. The so-called cross I could not avoid I may, for a change, take up with gladness. Might I not then, for the first time, be on the way to true discipleship?

The Lord who calls us will surely not leave us in confusion about what it is he asks. He knows perfectly well whether our desire to be a disciple, a learner, is an honest one. But still we worry. It seems a risky business, and what if we miss the way? What if we make the wrong decision? What if we take up crosses never meant for us? What if we fail to see the one appointed to us? What if . . . ?

"The care that is filling your mind at this moment," wrote George MacDonald,[49] "or but waiting till you lay the book aside to leap upon you—that need which is no need, is a demon sucking at the spring of your life.

"'No, mine is a reasonable care—an unavoidable care, indeed!'

"'Is it something you have to do this very moment?'

"'No.'

"'Then you are allowing it to usurp the place of something that is required of you this moment!'

"'There is nothing required of me at this moment.'

"'Nay, but there is—the greatest thing that can be required of man.'

"'Pray, what is it?'

"'Trust in the living God. . . .'

"'I do trust him in spiritual matters.'

"'Everything is an affair of the spirit. . . .'"

Here is the heart of the matter. We come to God for guidance in some practical affair, something we had not really thought of at all as an "affair of the spirit," but in his presence, as we pray, we come to see that it is in fact exactly that.

Why do we ask what we ask? Because we need it, of course. We've got to know. But then God looks at us as any father looks at his child, and in the recognition of his love we suddenly lose our frenzy. The words that were about to tumble out are silenced, and the thing we wanted looks different to us because we cannot help looking at it from his angle.

Asking God for a handout is one thing. We may get it. How often God simply hands things out right and left, to the good man and the bad man, to the man with faith and the man who hasn't an ounce of faith—good health and sun and rain and the capacity to enjoy and the ability to work and all sorts of "luck" for which he is not asked or ever thanked.

But when we understand the taking up of the cross in order to follow, we begin to understand that everything is actually an affair of the spirit, and we shall be asked about our motives. "The chief end of man," says the Shorter Catechism, "is to glorify God and enjoy him forever." This is what we are here for. Do I accept this position in God's universe or do I rebel against it?

The true disciple has a single eye. "Purity of heart," wrote Kierkegaard, "is to will one thing."[50] The glory of God is to be our primary motive. It should not surprise us then if what looked like a very simple thing (I don't ask very much, do I?) turns out to be a spiritual matter, an object that reveals my heart's direction.

"The LORD alone did lead him,"[51] was written about Israel. You can follow only one person at a time. Rushing off in all directions at once, trying to serve two masters, will ruin us. The sooner we make up our minds to take up the cross and follow one Lord and one Master, the sooner we will be shown the right road, the path of righteousness.

It is not reasonable to ask for guidance in one matter if we are aware that in another matter we have rejected the guidance already given. Let us first go back, if possible, to where we turned away. If this is no longer possible, let us confess our sin. It may often be a "small" thing in which we see we have been disobedient, while it is a "big" decision we are asking guidance for, but it is the big thing that has stopped us, brought us to attention, and forced us back to God. If he asks us then about something smaller, we are given the chance to correct it.

All our problems are theological ones, William Temple said. All of them have to do with our relationship to God and his to us, and this is precisely why it makes sense to come to God with them.

The taking up of the cross will mean sooner or later saying no to self. But it is also a resounding yes. It means saying yes when everything in us says no. To decide to do the thing that we (and it will seem everybody else in the world) do not want to do because it is not "natural." And in our giving of whole-hearted assent, we find to our amazement that the impossible becomes possible and the things we were sure were beyond us are now within reach, for God's command is his enabling. *Never* has he given an assignment that was not accompanied by the power to accomplish it.

The cross entails sacrifice, too. There is no getting around this. Christianity has been criticized and rejected by many as an "unnatural" religion, a life that denies living, a negation and not an affirmation. Jesus never tried to make it look easy. The principles he taught cut across the grain of human nature: lose your life in order to find it; be poor in spirit if you want to be happy; mourn if you want to rejoice; take the last place if you want the first. The corn of wheat must first fall into the ground and die if it is ever to produce anything.

What we must not forget is that he traveled this road before us. "He himself endured a cross and thought nothing of its shame"—not because he had a particular liking for self-denial and suffering but "because of the joy he knew would follow his suffering. . . . Think constantly of him enduring all that sinful men could say against him, and you will not lose your purpose or your courage."[52]

A few lines I learned while a student in college have come back to my mind, beckoning me when more immediate rewards were attracting my attention:

> I heard him call "Come follow."
> That was all.
> My gold grew dim, my soul went after him.
> Who would not follow
> If they heard him call?

4

the objectives

There is a sense in which the objective toward which God leads us is not separable from the means by which he will lead us there. The poet F. W. H. Myers recognized this when he wrote "St. Paul":

> Yea, through life, death, through sorrow and through sinning,
>   Christ shall suffice me, for He hath sufficed;
> Christ is the end, for Christ was the beginning,
>   Christ the beginning, for the end is Christ.

Christ, in other words, is the ultimate objective. Christ himself is also the way. This makes it difficult to have a chapter exclusively devoted to objectives. The things that are promised along the way (his presence, guidance, peace, light, assurance), and the conditions entailed by the promises are inextricably linked to the final object God has in mind. But being human, we cannot think of many things at once. So within the scope of this chapter, let us look at the goals of guidance as they are expressed in the Bible.

Our own goal is to know the right way. We don't like to make mistakes. What is the truth of the matter for me, right now? It's my life; I want to live it well. Or perhaps my decision affects people I care about—I want things to turn out well for them. Coming to God, we have come to the right place, for we have come to the One who not only can tell us the way, show us the truth, and give us life but who also has said, "I *am* the way, the truth, and the life."[1] Jesus identifies himself here in one of his great *I am* statements, and we are reminded of the primary condition of asking for help: the recognition of who God is. He is everything we are asking for. He is the Alpha, for nothing would have begun without him. He is the Omega, for it is in him that everything finds its perfection and fulfillment. These are mysteries that go deeper than we can fathom, but there are simpler terms which may help us.

Obviously we do not take a road unless it goes where we want to go. If we are following Christ, where is it he is taking us?

The Father's House

"To his holy abode" is one biblical answer to the question of where Christ is taking us. "Thou hast led in thy steadfast love the people whom thou hast redeemed, thou hast guided them by thy strength to thy holy abode."[2] The Father's house is where we belong, and the way to it, as in the story of the prodigal son, is repentance. So he leads us to the first objective. "God's kindness is meant to lead you to repentance."[3] Our relationship with him begins with this act of the will. "I will arise and go to my father."[4]

How do we get to him? Jesus Christ has told us. "I am the way."[5] We have free passage. This is a great theological truth we may hear often without much idea of its application in day-to-day living. A prayer written by Phillips Brooks has helped me to see that theology does work down where I live, that every event of every day is a chance to take a step toward God.

O Lord, by all thy dealings with us, whether of joy or pain, of light or darkness, let us be brought to thee. Let us value no treatment of thy grace simply because it makes us happy or because it makes us sad, because it gives us or denies us what we want; but may all that thou sendest us bring us to thee, that, knowing thy perfectness, we may be sure in every disappointment that thou art still loving us, and in every darkness that thou art still enlightening us, and in every enforced idleness that thou art still using us; yea, in every death that thou art still giving us life, as in his death thou didst give life to thy Son, our Savior, Jesus Christ. Amen.

"May all that thou sendest us bring us to thee." Or, to put it in another way, "This is the will of God, your sanctification."[6] Sanctification is an old word for making holy. All that redemption means, all that it takes to bring us home to God, is at one and the same time a part of the process of making us fit to live with him. "Thou wilt bring them in, and plant them on thy own mountain, the place, O LORD, which thou hast made for thy abode, the sanctuary, O LORD, which thy hands have established."[7] Nothing goes into the sanctuary except what is sanctified.

A simple little prayer like "Show me the way" or the more advanced but often glibly pronounced "Thy will be done" carries us far into regions we never meant to approach. We are wondering about the will of God in terms of changing jobs or buying a house or what courses to take in college, and we are told that the will of God is a matter of sanctification. The verse says, "your sanctification," using the plural "your." The process is not accomplished alone. "He led forth his people like sheep."[8] All God's people, all the flock he is shepherding, are in relationship to one another. What he does with one may seem puzzling to that one, but he has the whole flock in mind all the time, never forgetting, however, the individual. He names them, counts them, provides for them, and each has his own responsibility to the rest. All are made one, all are brought together under one Shepherd, in order that all may at last be holy.

"Holiness" is a frightening word only because of modern connotations. Originally it meant sound, whole (or "hale"), and happy. In the Old Testament the word meant set apart for a special purpose. What it takes to set a person apart for God's special purposes may not look at first glance like a way to soundness or happiness. Christ himself, we are told, had to be "sanctified" for the sake of those he loved.[9] Clearly this had nothing to do with the getting rid of sin, an idea we sometimes associate with sanctification. He was set apart for one purpose: "Lo, I come (in the volume of the book it is written of me) to do thy will, O God."[10] This meant, in his case, sacrifice. Not only his death on the cross but also many sacrifices before that. At the very beginning of his public ministry, as soon as he had been baptized and authenticated as the Son of God, he was "led up by the Spirit."[11] And where did that Spirit take him? Into green pastures and beside still waters? Not by any means. He was led into the wilderness. And he was led there, not to bask in the presence of God, but to be tempted by the devil.

Can the guidance of God actually take a person into a wilderness? It took Israel into one. It took them to Marah, where the water was too bitter to drink. It took Jesus into forty days and nights of harrowing temptation by his archenemy.

How such leading could possibly be the will of God for anyone, even for Jesus, would be a total mystery if we were to try to understand the case in isolation from others. But it was, according to Jesus' own words later, "for their sakes" that he sanctified himself.

We are not Jesus. We are not even a part of that huge mob of Israelites that moved through the deserts toward the promised land. But what we learn from them is meant for us, because we are going in the same direction—Home. I have found it true that obedience may lead me not to the fulfillment of my own ideals of spirituality but to very unexpected situations, very "unspiritual" situations, in my view, that are meant to teach me to be meek and lowly in heart. If I want to learn of him, this is what I am going to have to learn. And there, to my surprise, I find rest. I find the chance to recall once more (how many, many times I have to review my lessons) that if I am serious about my primary aim, I may be led elsewhere than my lesser aims would take me, for I do not know what I really need. God sees the "one thing needful," and he alone knows the path that will take me there.

His Name's Sake

When the prophet Elijah had called for a showdown with the prophets of Baal and had been answered by the miracle of fire from heaven, he began to see himself as a martyr and a hermit. The redoubtable Jezebel, for one, was after him and he ran for his life. Sitting under a broom tree, alone in the wilderness, he could see no solution to his problems but death. Death in itself did not scare him—if God would kill him, it looked to Elijah like a good way to go. But the idea of Jezebel's catching up with him turned his knees to water.

God's solution, however, was not death. Nothing so dramatic this time. Elijah had had plenty of theatrics in his lifetime (when God saw that they were what was needed for the good of his people and the sake of his name), but what he needed now were the simplest requirements of human life: rest and food. Elijah went to sleep and was wakened by an angel's touch. There in front of him was a cake baked on hot stones, and a jar of water. He didn't bother about the drama this time—though I think the question would have crossed *my* mind as to whether the angel had heated the stones and baked the cake himself. Elijah asked no questions. He merely ate and drank and went back to sleep.

The same thing happened a second time, and then Elijah had strength to take up the next leg of his journey. This was a long one—forty days and forty nights—that led to a cave where he again moaned his complaints to the Lord about being the only one left who was faithful. God sent wind, earthquake, and fire—the things a man of Elijah's temperament and experience would expect as manifestations of the Lord's presence with him—but this time the Lord was not in them. His voice came still and small, and he gave directions as to what Elijah was to do next.[12]

The accomplishment of God's objective for the nation of Israel required from Elijah not a tragic martyr's death in the wilderness but just sleep, and then cake and a jar of water delivered by an angel. The word of the Lord came not through a spectacular demonstration of power but in a whisper.

Elijah was in the wilderness not as Jesus was—because the Spirit had taken him there—but because his own fears had. Jesus was there in obedience to God. If we find ourselves in some lonely position, whether as a result of fear or obedience, God can still meet us there and work out his own purposes. But it may not come close to our idea of a spiritual solution. What we had thought of as the "glory of God" may seem to have disintegrated. "O Lord, thy will be done!" is a high-sounding prayer, but the lessons of meekness and lowliness of heart will probably take us to the bottom of the barrel. Elijah, the prophet who had four times called down fire from heaven, who parted water with his mantle, and who "went up by a whirlwind into heaven"[13]—this man, in the will of God, was also fed by ravens, by a destitute widow, and by an angel. He collapsed in exhaustion under a bush, his hopes demolished. But there the God he had once trusted was with him. It was all a part of the path of righteousness "for his name's sake."[14]

"If you were shipwrecked on a desert island, whom would you like to be your companion?" is a tired old question. For most of us, the idea of prolonged isolation with anybody we didn't love is a thing to be avoided at all cost. With someone we love it may look like heaven. With anyone else it looks like hell. We don't care to be "taken aside" or given any "quiet talks," to be subjected to any situation that will lead to heart-to-heart conversation, especially if the person holds any kind of power over us. We'd rather stick with the crowd. The presence of other people is a protection. Issues can more easily be avoided.

I have sometimes been afraid to be alone with God. This fear, John tells us, would be "cast out" if I loved God perfectly, but of course I don't. Issues I have been successfully avoiding might come up if I were to get alone with him. I know quite well that something awkward may arise between us that I would just as soon not deal with. But what if the kind Shepherd takes me aside somewhere because he has something special for me, something he did not want to bring out until he got me alone?

When Jesus was in the region called the Decapolis, a deaf and dumb man was brought to him for healing.[15] Quite a crowd had collected to see the fun, but what Jesus planned to do he wanted to do in private. What if the man had said, "Oh, no, you don't get me off by myself!" But the deaf-mute was willing to take the risk. What he had heard of Jesus gave him hope; he took him at his word and got healed.

The healing was not meant, however, as a public demonstration. Not that time. Jesus wanted it kept quiet. This in itself indicates that the divine objective is not necessarily what we think ("Wouldn't it be a marvelous testimony!"). Jesus told people not to mention it but, as we probably would have done, they spread it around as fast as they could. On another occasion, Jesus took a blind man by the hand and led him away from the village before healing him. He wanted to get the man alone. Then he told him not to go back to the village at all, but straight home.[16]

There can be no doubt that Jesus had good reasons for wanting certain things kept confidential. Sir Robert Anderson, who was for many years head of Scotland Yard and therefore must have been thoroughly experienced in sifting out truth and discovering the real issues at stake, wrote, "Among Christians it is pestilently evil to make the exceptional experience of some the rule of faith for all. The Word of God is our guide and not the experience of fellow-Christians; and when this is ignored the consequences are disastrous."[17] People have a strong tendency to make of some spiritual experiences status symbols. Doing this is to forget what God's objective is—it is not our reputation he is concerned about. We ought to be willing to allow God to do "special" things for us if he wants to and to accept them quietly, confident that whatever he does fits into the working out of his purposes for us all. Our sanctification is at the very least an intricate business, and who are we to say that advertising is necessarily helpful?

Help for Others

In fulfilling his objective of "bringing many sons to glory"[18] (another of the biblical ways of describing his objective), God often chooses one of those sons to bring another one. He gives to us in order that we may give to others. But this is not the same as saying that what he gives us he will give to others. A song that has been popular among American Christians says, "What he's done for others he'll do for you." If this refers to his receiving us, it's true. He receives all who come. But the song is misleading if it is taken to mean that *whatever* God has done for others he will do for you. He did not make all deaf men hear or all blind men see. He got Paul and Silas out of prison, but he left John the Baptist in prison—left him there, in fact, until his head was chopped off. He prevents some accidents and allows others. He keeps us from diseases at times and at other times lets us get them. When he lets us get them he sometimes heals us and sometimes lets us die. But in whatever he does in the course of our lives, he gives us, through the experience, some power to help others.

This ability to share is one of his intermediate objectives: "And the LORD will guide you continually, and satisfy your desire with good things, and make your bones strong; and you shall be like a watered garden, like a spring of water, whose waters fail not."[19] We need to remember that if we are asking for something that will end with us or shut us off from others, a dead-end kind of thing we have prayed for without much regard for our responsibility to other people, it may be withheld. On the other hand it may, like the quails sent to the Israelites in the wilderness because they begged for meat, be granted, along with leanness of soul.[20] That leanness, that impoverishment, inevitably accompanies selfishness. There is no way to Life except through the narrow gate, but this narrow gate opens out into unimagined largeness and fullness of being. But if we choose the broad way and the wide gate which makes room for our selfish wants, we will find someday that the lane ends, as on a modern highway, we have no place to "squeeze" left or right, and there will be leanness and finally destruction.

Commitment (A Parenthesis)

If we have chosen the narrow gate, it is fortunate for us that we cannot always find a way to go back. We are committed—we have trusted God and agreed with his objective, though we do not know all that this is going to mean.

An early lesson in commitment is a ride in a roller coaster. Most of us remember the eager waiting at the gate, the rush to climb in when the cars came clattering to a stop at the platform, the ecstasy with which we gripped the cold steel of the guardrail in front of us, and the first steep climb up into the sky. But in that split second when we came over the top and saw the tracks dropping away beneath us, we gasped at what we were about to do. The impossibility of changing our minds was an awful revelation. As I look back on it, it strikes me as appalling that so many are willing to pay to have themselves helplessly flung through the air like this, sickeningly plunged and whirled and jerked. The worst of it, the part that doesn't bother many children, is that the train isn't going anywhere. You've had this terrible ride just for the *ride*.

As we grow up, we are usually more careful not to commit ourselves unless there is a destination we want to reach. We've learned that getting there may not be fun.

The initial choice to go the whole way with God is made of necessity in ignorance of all that will follow. We have been warned that the road will be a hard one, for our Master himself walked a hard road, and he reminds us that servants are not greater than their masters. To the scribe who so eagerly affirmed his willingness to follow anywhere Jesus might lead, Jesus said, "Foxes have holes, and birds of the air have nests; but the Son of man has nowhere to lay his head."[21]

But if, given all these previews of what is coming, we have nevertheless set our faces to follow the Pioneer of Faith, there will be many times along the road when we look over our shoulder, longing, like the Israelites on the way to the promised land, for the "leeks, the onions, and the garlic" of our slavery.[22] We are fortunate, then, that it is hard to find a way back.

"Our heart is not turned back . . . though thou hast sore broken us in the place of dragons, and covered us with the shadow of death."[23] It has usually happened that a place God has put me has proved to be (sometimes quite in contrast to my expectation) a place of contentment. I have looked at others and said, "How do they stand it?" and then, finding myself in a similar place, in the will of God, I had the answer. It is a great thing to know you are where you belong.

But one particular spot where I lived as a missionary became like a "place of dragons." It was full of things I was afraid of and did not know how to cope with. Once in a while I felt as though I were about to be devoured. "Sore broken" is the psalmist's expression, and I thought I knew how he felt. I was on my way back to that place one night, camping where we usually did at the junction of two rivers. The Indians had made me a reed hut to sleep in and had finished their own hut-building, fishing, eating, and talking. Everything was quiet except for the night birds and tree frogs. There was nothing especially distinct about this journey back home. I had made it before. But as I lay in my blanket I began to feel something like what fell on Abraham: "a horror of great darkness." How could I go back to those "dragons"? My heart was about to turn back.

Then I thought of Jesus' words to his disciples: "Lo, I am with you all the days."[24] If he was with me then I was certainly with him. The place of dragons was the place he was taking me, and I was still following—I had not gotten off the track. I was with him still, sharing in a small measure his cross.

"Thou hast covered us with the shadow of death." That dark shadow that chills us may be, after all, the shadow of the cross. His mercy and his love surround us still. It is this mercy and this love, although we do not always realize it, that keep our hearts from turning back. Never for a second does God lose sight of his objective. It is we who forget what it is. We are distracted by immediate circumstances, and it is no wonder we want to give up the whole thing. It was the "joy that was set before him" that enabled Jesus to endure the cross.[25]

Without a clear understanding of the ultimate objective, the intermediate objectives make no sense to us. "Why this, Lord?" we keep asking. But if we bear in mind that we shall, beyond any doubt whatsoever, finally dwell in the house of the Lord, settle down to stay in his presence, then the intermediate pastures and waters, even the valley of the shadow or the place of dragons, are understood. They are stations and landings along the journey, and they will not last long.

Thanksgiving

It is even possible to be thankful for the valley of the shadow, not because we like it or find anything to enjoy in that fearsome ravine but because we have been told ahead of time that it is not the end of the journey. It is on the way to the Lord's house, and when we get there we'll know it was worth enduring any trouble along the way.

The chances are, however, that while we happen to be in the middle of the trouble it doesn't look like anything but trouble. It doesn't occur to us to compare it with the biblical illustrations, and if someone suggested we do this, we might laugh. "You want me to think spiritually about *this?* Why, it's got nothing to do with the will of God or the path of righteousness or any of that. It's nothing but bad luck."

The Scriptures have a way of covering all the possibilities. Our bad luck can be transformed if we do one simple thing: "Give thanks in all circumstances; for this is the will of God in Christ Jesus for you."[26] That is what the Bible says. We could not ask for a clearer statement. The circumstances may not look even remotely like the will of God, but to give thanks in (not necessarily for) them is the will of God. That much we can do.

The Knowledge of Truth

The God of Truth purposes that all men should come to the knowledge of the truth. This is another facet of his ultimate objective. We know that the truth will make us free, but not just any truth acquired anyhow and anytime. The leading of God toward the full light of truth is, like our recognition of him, a lifelong process, and for this we can be thankful. We move one step at a time, and Christ is the Way and the Truth. He does not drop the whole block of truth into our laps at once, for we could not possibly bear the weight of it. .

The words "You shall know the truth and the truth shall make you free" are so familiar that those which preceded them are often skipped over entirely: "If you continue in my word." This is a very different thing from "If you fully comprehend and are perfectly obedient to all I have said." The promise is to those who go on learning; it may be only a very little at a time. "If you continue in my word, you are truly my disciples, and you will know the truth, and the truth will make you free."[27] Discipleship, which means discipline, is the only road to freedom. We walk by faith now, for we do not see all the truth. Even Paul admitted that he knew only in part and saw through a glass darkly. But truth is God's objective, and when the day comes for it to be fully revealed, faith will no longer be needed.

We will know the truth in the end, because in the beginning we have taken that first simple step, asking God to show us his will. "If any man's will is to do his will, he shall know. . . ." "Obedience," George MacDonald said, "is the opener of eyes."[28]

We have a Helper, too. "When the Spirit of truth comes, he will guide you into all the truth."[29]

As a child in the second or third grade, I was having trouble with arithmetic. I tried very hard in school to understand, and I did my homework diligently every night, often asking my father to explain things I had missed in class. But the lessons were so hard for me that I lay awake at night crying for fear I would fail. One day the teacher said, "If there is anything you don't understand, ask me. That's what I'm here for, you know."

I shall never forget the enormous relief that simple statement brought to me. It had never occurred to me, and I suppose she thought it was so obvious to us she didn't need to say it, but the logic of it hit me: that *was* what she was there for. Why else was she called a teacher? And she was there to teach *me*.

God has given us a teacher. That is why we have the Holy Spirit. "When the Spirit of truth comes, he will guide you into all the truth." "If any of you lack wisdom, let him ask of God."[30]

When we contemplate the great ends God has in mind for us, it may be that the thing which brings us to him today seems so trivial as to be hardly worth mentioning to him. What business have we got troubling the Master with this little worldly concern? But we may hope our concerns are not littler or more worldly than the things we read of in the Bible that brought all kinds of people to him. He is a Master used to being troubled by ordinary people, willing to be bothered by our stumbling, grade-school efforts, so long as we bring them to him. For then, meeting us where we are (and where else would he get hold of us?) he can take us on further. He never loses sight of his own object, which is of far greater importance to him than any of our objects are to us.

Most of us do things every day that we do not particularly enjoy doing. We do them in order to accomplish some object we desire. A man may not enjoy the actual pushing of a lawn mower, but he does like to see the lawn neat. A woman may find peeling potatoes less than satisfying in itself, but she loves to see her family enjoy a good meal. T. H. White, who wrote *The Once and Future King*, said of an earlier book, "I shall probably be glad to have written this book, but I hate writing it."

The men who got to the top of Mt. Everest got there through literal peril, toil, and pain, but they stood one day on the peak. They would not have suffered what they suffered if they had not had that hope in them. It would be quite true, I think, to say also they *could* not have suffered it—it would have been beyond human power, unless they had had a supremely desired object.

It will help us to do what we have to do today if we can remember why we do it, especially if it seems to us that the answer we get when we pray for the will of God is beyond our powers. It is then that we need to look beyond our powers, beyond ourselves, beyond our own immediate desires. Let us go over again in our minds God's objectives, and we may be surprised at the ease with which we can then obey.

The consciousness of his origin and destiny enabled Jesus to do very humdrum things. We get things completely backward when we feel that because of "who we are" or "where we came from" or what an important job we have to do we can't stop or stoop to do the humdrum; we are engaged in the high and holy will of God and can't be bothered with the ordinary. A look at how humdrum it must have been for the Son of God to become the Son of man will help us to regain a proper perspective. His whole human life was a humiliation. And at the Last Supper, we read, Jesus, "well aware . . . that he had come from God and was going back to God . . . taking a towel . . . began to wash the disciples' feet."[31] It was the act of a slave, just before the final humiliation of crucifixion, but he did it voluntarily, remembering his origin and his destiny.

We, too, come from God, and it is back to God we go.

5

the means

I said in the introduction that this is not a how-to-get-it book. Much more is involved in following the Lord's leading than a list of his methods. We need to know what is promised, what are the conditions of the promises, and what is God's object. An understanding of those things will put us in a position to discern his will in a particular situation.

How, then, does God go about showing us what we are to do?

Supernatural Means

Visible Signs

We think first of cloud, fire, and a star. Visible phenomena were the means of showing people in the Bible where God wanted them to go. The pillar of cloud and fire never left the children of Israel. Most of us, when we are searching for guidance, envy them with all our hearts. Here was a visible, nondebatable sign: "by day in a pillar of cloud to lead them along the way, and by night in a pillar of fire to give them light, that they might travel by day and by night."[1] There it was, always in the sky, and they knew that the Lord was in it. No room was left for argument as to what they were meant to do. "Throughout all their journeys, whenever the cloud was taken up from over the tabernacle, the people of Israel would go onward; but if the cloud was not taken up, then they did not go onward till the day that it was taken up."[2] As simple as red and green lights.

Then there was the star of Bethlehem. No one is sure who those wise men or astrologers were, or how many of them there were, or how far they had traveled, but they knew enough about the stars to recognize a new one when it appeared, and somehow they knew what it signified. They called it "his star," and they knew it heralded the birth of a King of the Jews. The star apparently moved. They had seen it in the east and it "went in front of them until at last it shone immediately above the place where the little child lay. The sight of the star filled them with indescribable joy."[3] If we are ever tempted to wonder whether God can possibly communicate with people who seem to us remote and unlikely prospects, if we doubt his ability to choose a method to suit the individuals involved, if we think of world events as rather haphazard and of specific points in time and space as hardly worth his notice, it will do us good to remember those mysterious strangers and that star.

Audible Signs

Sometimes instead of a visible sign, God gave an audible one. The Philistines were arrayed against David in the valley of Rephaim. When David asked God's permission to attack, he was told to wait until he heard "the sound of marching in the tops of the balsam trees."[4] That sound in that place could only be supernatural. There were many occasions when "the word of the Lord came"—a voice, clearly heard, clearly understood, clearly identified.

Angels

Then, of course, there were angels. A study of both the visible and the audible manifestations of angels in the stories of the Bible will probably surprise most of us, for they are not rare as we usually think of them. The Christmas story alone includes five angelic visitations. The first time an angel came to a human being, according to the biblical record, it was to an outcast Egyptian servant woman, Hagar, who, the angel said, was to be the mother of Ishmael. Abraham had many encounters with angels. Lot, Jacob, Balaam, David, Elijah, Zechariah, Mary, Joseph, Peter, and Paul all met angels sent on particular errands from the Lord. They came quite unexpectedly (it was not that the man or woman to whom they came had been praying for a supernatural visitor, or even for guidance), and the message they brought was often a startling one, one that quite changed the program.

Philip, for example, was preaching the gospel in Samaritan villages when an angel arrived and said abruptly, "Get up and go south."[5] If Philip had not obeyed, he would have missed the opportunity to give the good news about Jesus to an important foreign official who "happened" to be traveling home to Ethiopia. (I am afraid some of my requests for guidance come out of a desire for something interesting and unusual such as an opportunity to speak to an important person, rather than for strength to do the ordinary duty, which in Philip's case was preaching in those little villages. But his doing the duty made him eligible for the interesting and unusual opportunity he didn't ask for.)

It was not only to men engaged in the Lord's business that angels came. Lot does not give me the impression of a man working overtime for God. Yet he is called a "righteous" man,[6] and when God was about to destroy Sodom, he sent angels to rescue Lot and his family. Lot took the angels' warning seriously enough to tell his sons-in-law to get themselves and their wives out of the city. But when they received this suggestion with mild amusement, Lot dallied, taking the divine warning with a grain of salt. When a second urging failed to rouse him, the angels "seized him and his wife and his two daughters by the hand, the Lord being merciful to him, and they brought him forth and set him outside the city."[7] I would call this coercion, but it was a merciful coercion, and it lasted only up to a point. Lot was plunked down out of range of the brimstone, and from there he was on his own and told to run for his life. (God's sovereignty and man's responsibility are illuminated in this story—Lot was first dragged, then had to run on his own two legs.)

Lot's experience is very different from the picture of the green pastures, still waters, and gentle Shepherd. But the mercy of God shows itself in a thousand different ways, and he knows who it is he is dealing with. If it takes only a flicker of an eye for the servant who awaits his master's bidding, God can give that. If it takes a rude yank to bring a man to his senses, God knows how to deliver that just as well.

Peter, chained in prison for preaching the gospel and fully expecting to be executed as James had been, was rescued by an angel. A light flashed, the angel gave the prisoner a poke and said, "Get up." He led Peter past two sets of guards, through an iron gate, down one street, and then, like Lot, Peter was on his own. Only then did he realize he wasn't dreaming.

My father, when he was a small boy, was climbing on an upper story of a house that was being built. He walked to the end of a board that he thought was nailed at the other end. It wasn't. Slowly it began to tip. He knew he was doomed, but inexplicably the board began to tip the other way, as though a hand had pushed it down again. He always wondered whether it was an angel's hand.

A blind man my father knew was about to step into what he thought was his cabin on board ship. It was in fact a hatchway, but he felt a hand on his chest pushing him back. He asked who was there. There was no answer. Was an angel sent to rescue him?

I have never forgotten hearing Dr. Virginia Blakeslee of Africa tell how angels delivered her from hostile people (I think she said they were cannibals). She did not know at the time what it was that drove them back as they charged into the clearing where her hut was. She only knew that as she was praying and they were dancing around the hut with their weapons in their hands, something made them flee. This happened on several different nights. Finally the leader of the group came to her in the daytime asking to be allowed to see the men who were guarding her. Bewildered, she said there was no one. The man searched her hut and, finding nothing, described to her the strong men with swords who had come out of her door as the cannibals danced.

G. K. Chesterton said that the most wonderful thing about miracles is that they do sometimes happen. There are certainly many things for which we have no explanation. Why should not God send his angels to do things for him in the twentieth century? Do centuries make any difference to the Eternal God?

Dreams and Visions

Another method God has often used to guide men is dreams and visions. Since Freud interpreted dreams as coming from the depths of man's subconscious, signifying his fears, anxieties, and suppressed desires, we have almost forgotten the possibility that God might take over the subconscious long enough to show a man something he might not see while conscious. In simpler times men assumed that dreams showed not the darkness of their own hearts but the light they needed. The Indians of Ecuador believe this, and their witch doctors drink herbs that produce visions (we would prefer to call them hallucinations, I suppose) of great importance. After drinking the "ghost vine," a witch doctor in Arajuno, the station manned by Ed McCully, saw that Ed had been killed. Several days later the vision was confirmed. Word reached Arajuno that Ed had been speared to death by Aucas.

But this is a book about the guidance of God. Can the hallucinations of a jungle witch doctor have anything to do with this? I don't know. As to whether Almighty God could have reason for letting a man like that in on classified information, I have no idea. What we do know is that the subconscious mind is one channel by which man receives messages, whether they come from television, drugs, demons, or (as they often did in the Bible accounts) from God.

Jacob saw angels and a ladder in his dream and was assured of God's presence and the promise of great progeny. Joseph had prophetic dreams he would have done well to keep to himself, since they sent his

brothers into paroxysms of jealousy. Gideon found out what he ought
to do through another man's dream. (And it was only by chance that
he overheard the man telling it. Do God's methods sometimes strike
us as whimsical or careless?)

The irascible king Nebuchadnezzar had a dream which worried
him very much, but he required that his wise men tell him both the
dream and its interpretation. It was an exile from Judah named Daniel
who got the answer—and he got it through a dream of his own. "No
wise men, enchanters, magicians, or astrologers can show to the king
the mystery which the king has asked," Daniel said, "but there is a
God in heaven who reveals mysteries. . . . But as for me, not because
of any wisdom that I have more than all the living has this mystery
been revealed to me. . . ."[8] Daniel did not doubt that God was the
giver of his dream.

Paul had a vision one night in Troas of a man beseeching him
to come over into Macedonia. He and his companions set sail immediately, "concluding that God had called us to preach the gospel
to them." Another time, while praying in the temple, he fell into a
trance and saw the Lord telling him to get out of Jerusalem.[9] It looks
as though Paul was used to taking his dreams seriously.

Prophets

Guidance came to God's people also through prophets. These were
men of widely differing temperaments and personalities who were
inspired—in-breathed—by the Spirit of God. How often we read
this artless introduction in the Old Testament: "The word of the Lord
came to me saying. . . ." We are not told how the word came, or how
they knew it was the Lord who spoke, but it came, and they knew
who was speaking, and they put down what he said.

When Jehoshaphat, the king of Judah, was going to join his counter-
part, Ahab king of Israel, in war, he wanted to find the will of the Lord
for a battle decision. So Ahab called together four hundred prophets.
"Attack," they said. But Jehoshaphat wasn't satisfied. He felt he needed
the advice of one more. Micaiah was brought and prophesied defeat.

For that, Ahab promptly put Micaiah in prison on bread and water. Micaiah was right, but it wasn't what the king wanted to hear.[10]

Jeremiah was dropped into a pit of slime for prophesying things that were too discouraging.[11] It is understandable that the job of a prophet has never been a particularly coveted one. The word of the Lord is likely to inconvenience us.

The word of the Lord got in the way of Balaam. He was so bent on doing his own will that it took the ass he was riding on to see the angel of the Lord blocking the road and to speak in a voice that got his attention.[12] Whatever our categories for the means God may use to get through to us, they had better include donkeys.

Years ago I heard Gladys Aylward, called in her biography The Small Woman, tell how she was once in desperate need of money, traveling through the mountains of China. The party came to a tunnel that the muleteer refused to pass through because it was known to be inhabited by demons. Finally he agreed to go through, but only on one condition: that she would make enough noise to frighten the demons. Miss Aylward sang hymns at the top of her voice (and I know she had a very big voice for such a little person). When they got to the other end, she heard the sound of wind in the leaves, and in the sound of the wind there was a voice. The voice of a demon, of course, thought the muleteer, and he sank to his knees in terror.

"It's nothing to do with you!" cried Gladys Aylward. "This is *my* God, speaking to *me!*" And she told us what God had to say: "Ye have not, because ye ask not."[13] It was only then that she realized she had not once prayed for the money she needed. A woman of faith and prayer, she had been so preoccupied with other things that she had entirely forgotten the simplest solution to her need. The story ends with the money being provided in nearly as supernatural a way as the voice had come to her.

These examples are enough to illustrate what we would call the supernatural means. They may seem to us to have been used only in far-off times or faraway places, but this may be only because we ourselves are living, like the prodigal son, in a far country, trying to forget all about the Father's house. It is much more in keeping with Christian faith and with Christian intelligence to acknowledge the possibility of miracles anywhere, anytime.

But there is one thing we ought to notice about these miracles. When God guided by means of the pillar of cloud and fire, by the star of Bethlehem, by visitations of angels, by the word coming through visions and dreams and prophets and even through an insulted donkey, in most cases these were not signs that had been asked for. And when they were asked for, as in the case of Jehoshaphat and Ahab, they were not accepted.

Supernatural phenomena were given at the discretion of the divine wisdom. It is not for us to ask that God will guide us in some miraculous way. If, in his wisdom, he knows that such means are what we need, he will surely give them, as he gave one to Miss Aylward in the extremity of her need. But it is significant that the word she heard in the wind was a Scripture verse. It took an audible voice to remind her of it, but it was one she knew by heart.

I have never heard any voices or seen any visions from heaven, but I have been reminded "out of the blue" on more occasions than I can count, of some word from the Bible that exactly suited my need. At other times the word has been given through the reading for that day—the part of the Bible I had come to in regular reading, or the psalm for the day according to the church calendar, or the verses in the little book called *Daily Light*, which is nothing more than a selection of Scripture arranged for each day of the year.

When a shortwave radio message told me many years ago that my husband and four friends were missing in the jungle, the words of Isaiah 43:1–3 came to me almost as if they had been spoken aloud, but they were words I had memorized years before: "Fear not: for I have redeemed thee, I have called thee by thy name; thou art mine. When thou passest through the waters, I will be with thee; and through the rivers, they shall not overflow thee: when thou walkest through the fire, thou shalt not be burned; neither shall the flame kindle upon thee.

For I am the LORD thy God." These old words came with a power and an insistence that convinced me they came from God, and with them came the faith to believe they were true. However the word comes to our attention, if it is God's truth for us at the time, we are given that assurance.

There is a second thing to notice about the extraordinary means. They came in the ordinary course of events. People were going about their usual business when God broke in in a special way. The supernatural occurred in conjunction with the natural.

Natural Means

Duty

We are going along in life, doing the usual things, when suddenly we come up against a thing we are not sure about. We need guidance. The temptation is to stop everything and ask for a sign. Once in a while this is the thing to do. Gideon did it when he put out his fleece, asking that on the first night it should be wet with dew while the ground around remained dry and that the opposite should happen on the second night. But far more often we find God leading men while they are doing what they normally are supposed to do. David was taking care of sheep, the boy Samuel was serving in the temple, Matthew was collecting taxes, when the Lord called them.

"Do the next thing" is one of the best pieces of advice I have ever had. It works in any kind of situation and is especially helpful when we don't know what to do. What if we don't even know what the "next thing" is? We can find something. Some duty lies on our doorstep. The rule is DO IT. The doing of that thing may open our eyes to the next.

I feel a little wistful now and then that God leaves so much up to me. The exercise of the intelligence is taxing. Couldn't I just shut my eyes and ask for a vision? This was not how it happened with Paul or the others. When Paul saw the vision of the man from Macedonia, he had been traveling. In ancient times, travel must surely have been at least as wearing as it is today. Paul and Timothy had done the walking and the talking and the sailing and negotiating and searching and bargaining for passage, food, and lodging their journey required. They were, I imagine, bone-weary. They had gone to bed, I hope, somewhere. Whether Paul had gone to sleep or was lying staring into the darkness of some drafty, noisy inn we don't know. But God was with him there, his Companion in the normal course of life, and in the way God himself chose, he issued instructions for the next move.

Timing

It is reasonable to expect that God will use whatever means may be appropriate *at the time*. The time I refer to is God's time, not ours. We will know when we need to know, not before.

When I review "all the way which the Lord my God hath led me"[14]—those segments of the way I can remember because they seemed to me significant—I realize that nearly all of my trouble with finding out the will of God came because I wanted it too soon. I like to plan. I like to have things mapped out well in advance, and uncertainty of any sort puts me on edge. Perhaps it is for this very reason God has often asked me to wait until the last minute, right up to what looked like the screaming edge, before I found out what he wanted me to do. My acceptance of his timing was a rigorous exercise in trust. I was tempted to charge the Lord with negligence and inattention, like the disciples in the boat in a storm. They toiled frantically until the situation became impossible, and then instead of asking for Jesus' help they yelled, "Master, don't you care that we're drowning?"[15] They weren't perishing, they were panicking. It was not too late. Jesus got up and merely spoke to the wind and sea.

On that other occasion, many centuries earlier, when the power of God to command water was what was needed to lead his people, the priests of Israel actually had to get their feet wet before God did anything. Why does he put us to this kind of test? Probably to give us the chance to make a conscious act of faith, often a specific, physical act, a move of some kind toward him. "And when . . . the feet of the priests bearing the ark were dipped in the brink of the water . . . the waters coming down from above stood and rose up in a heap. . . ."[16]

One of my most crucial decisions concerned my going to a tribe of Indians called Aucas. This tribe had killed my husband and four other men, and the idea of a woman attempting to do what they couldn't do was preposterous. However, not seeing how I could evade it, I put my life on the line, praying only, "Lord, here I am. If you want me to go, you'll have to make a way." For once, I had no suggestions to offer as to how he might make it. In fact, I felt pretty sure he wouldn't. But at night I would wake and think about it: what on earth I would do if a chance came to make contact with the tribe, and how serious a matter it was because it was not just my own life that would have to be considered but also that of my small daughter, and what kind of God would ask a mother to do such a thing? My mind would go round and round these questions and in and out until it was a hopeless tangle. I would always ask desperately to be shown God's will, but he never showed it to me *until the time came.* And when it came, it was as clear as the sunlight. What to do was all mapped out for me exactly, and I had a matter of minutes to make up my mind to do it.[17]

Sometimes, though, we are in a quandary because we have already been shown what we ought to do and we are not satisfied with it. We are saying, "Lord, when are you going to tell me?" and the truth is that he has told us.

Moses, having been told plainly that God would not permit him to cross Jordan, asked again if he might. "Let it suffice you; speak no more to me of this matter," the Lord said. "You shall not go over this Jordan."[18]

Our difficulty, like Moses', is that we can't accept what has been told us. But there is no use praying any more about it.

Sometimes the word comes very slowly. In Psalm 112:4 (RSV) we read, "Light rises in the darkness for the upright." It might be a gradual thing, imperceptible at first as the coming of the dawn, but long before we see it, the cock crows and there are stirrings. There is no question at all that the dawn will come. We have only to wait.

When a woman named Ruth sought the advice of her mother-in-law, Naomi, as to what the next step should be in relation to her kinsman Boaz, the answer Naomi gave her is one that has given me great comfort in puzzling situations: "Sit still, my daughter, until thou know how the matter will fall."[19]

Habakkuk was one of those reluctant Old Testament prophets who saw things he had no desire to see and was therefore bound to speak God's message about them to the people. But it was not by any means an easy thing to sort out of these horrors what he ought to say. "I will take my stand to watch," he wrote, "and station myself on the tower, and look forth to see what he will say to me, and what I will answer concerning my complaint. And the LORD answered me: 'Write the vision; make it plain upon tablets, so he may run who reads it. For still the vision awaits its time; it hastens to the end—it will not lie. If it seem slow, wait for it; it will surely come, it will not delay. Behold, he whose soul is not upright in him shall fail, but the righteous shall live by his faith.'"[20]

God Calls Us by Name

It is said that the sweetest sound in any language is the sound of one's own name. People who engage in public relations know the importance of using a person's name. Whether we call people by name at all and what name we use are deeply significant and are often a dead giveaway of our attitude toward a person. We have, for example, a clue to the kind of relationship that exists in a marriage when we hear the partners call each other "sweetheart" or "mommy" and "daddy." And what of the mental postures revealed by calling a man "Dr. Smith," plain "Smith," "Bill," or "old what's-his-name"?

In an airport, most of us pay little attention to the announcements coming over the public address system, precisely because it is only the public that is being addressed. But if we hear our own name, we come to life very quickly.

I once took a little dog through a course in obedience school. One of the lessons he had to learn was to respond only to my voice. There were forty-nine other dogs and their masters in the circle, and commands were given by more than one person at a time, so each dog had to distinguish, out of all the noise, the one voice that called to him.

Sheep, too, know the voice of the shepherd and will not follow a stranger. "He calls his own sheep by name and leads them out," John tells us.[21] The Shepherd of our souls issues a personal call, in recognition of our individuality.

When Mary went to the garden tomb on the first Easter morning, she did not know the Lord right away. She took him to be the gardener until he spoke her name. That brought recognition. Instantly she responded, "Master!"[22] (And we know by those two forms of address, "Mary" and "Master," something important about their relationship.)

In Isaiah we read, "Thus saith the LORD that created thee, . . . I have called thee by thy name; thou art mine."[23]

How shall we hear that call? Is it likely that we shall actually hear a voice speaking our name? We cannot deny that some have. Paul was stopped in his tracks on the road to Damascus by a light and a voice. John, on the island of Patmos, saw a vision and heard a voice. The boy Samuel was awakened from sleep in the temple by the Lord's voice calling his name. Elijah heard a voice even though it was still and small. Some in our own day have heard voices, we are told, but I am not one of them. There has never come to me anything audible. But I have found that the Lord knows how to call us. (Strange that I should be surprised at that!) He knows the best way to get our attention, and if we are ready to listen or to be shown, we will hear or see whatever it is he has chosen as his means.

A dear old Scottish lady whom I used to call my "Canadian mom" told me several years after her husband's death how she had realized ways she might have been a better wife to him. She said to the Lord then, "Why didn't you show me, Lord?" He answered, "Ah, but you weren't ready to be shown!"

I loved that story because it showed me her humility (such a godly lady, not ready to be shown?) and the depth of her desire to do the will of God. But it also delighted me to know that the Lord had spoken to her in a Scottish accent.

A friend of my husband told him how God had answered his prayer for a new secretary. A young woman called him on the telephone, and as she was talking, the story went, "The Holy Spirit said to me as plain as I'm talking to you now, 'That's her!'"

Maybe the Lord makes mistakes in grammar. Why should it matter? The point is that he speaks our language. This was astonishing to the Quichua Indians. Could they really pray in Quichua instead of Spanish? Yes. God understood them. And there came a day when he spoke to them in Quichua. We began to translate the Bible, and then for the first time some of them woke up and said, "God speaks to me!"

"The sheep follow him: for they know his voice."[24]

It is possible of course, because we are human, to be mistaken. I may think I have heard his voice when I haven't, but he is still my Shepherd and will call me back.

There are moments in our lives (and how we wish there were many more of them) when we are given certainty that outshines everything else. An old German hymn writer (my copy of the hymn gives only the initials "T. S. M.") described this certainty:

> No other voice than Thine has ever spoken,
>   O Lord, to me—
> No other words but Thine the stillness broken
>   Of life's lone sea.
> There openeth the spirit's silent chamber
>   No other hand—
> No other lips can speak the language tender,
>   Speech of the Fatherland.
> For others speak to one the eye beholdeth,
>   Who veils the soul within—
> Some know not all the joy, and all the sorrow,
>   And none know all the sin.

> They speak to one they love, it may be blindly,
>   Or hate, as it may be,
> They speak but to the shadow, the illusion:
>   Thou speakest Lord, to *me*.

On looking back we can tell, I think, that although many other voices called and confused us and perhaps convinced us for a time, they never broke the stillness of that inner sea, never really reached the "spirit's silent chamber."

It is a temptation for us, as it was for my dog in obedience school, to look around to see what others are doing. Simon Peter had this trouble, too, when, after that wonderful breakfast on the beach cooked by the resurrected Lord, Jesus asked him to follow him. "Lord, what about this man?" Peter wanted to know. "What is that to you?" Jesus answered. "*You* follow me."[25] Most of us will have all we can handle if we do that. We had better not get sidetracked wondering what kind of progress others are making.

Human Agents

We have considered in an earlier chapter how God guides his people always in relationship to one another, like a flock. This is perhaps one of the most important things to remember when we are looking for personal guidance. We ought to look first of all to those with whom we have some special relationship.

The divine order is hierarchy. There are different levels of being, and different positions in human relations that are God-given and cannot safely be ignored. The Bible uses the figures of father-son, king-subject, master-slave, teacher-pupil, and husband-wife to illustrate spiritual principles. We are told to be subject to one another. We must obey civil authorities (Jesus paid his taxes), wives must be subject to their husbands, children are to obey their parents in the Lord.[26] We need to be sure we are obeying the rules in these matters before we start seeking some more mystical guidance. The chances are very good that the will of God for a student in an institution, for example, is obedience to the authority of that institution. The will of God for a wife may be simply the cheerful doing of what her husband would like to do.

There are exceptions. "To obey God rather than men" is an over-worked verse.[27] We ought to have reached a high plane of spiritual perception before we invoke that one. Most of us will have a hard enough time rendering to Caesar the things that are Caesar's before we are spiritually competent to start handing over to God what is normally Caesar's. Jesus had some biting words for the Pharisees who encouraged men to give to God what properly belonged to their parents. In this they were "making void the word of God."[28]

God works always with perfect wisdom, always with perfect love, and nearly always in conjunction with human means. He led the people of Israel, but he gave them a human leader. He revealed himself to Moses directly, gave his instructions directly to him, but also used other intermediaries to lead Moses. "Now go, lead the people to the place of which I have spoken to you," God said; "behold, my angel shall go before you."[29] God, the angel, the man, the people—this was the order by which the guidance came, and the people in their turn were chosen to bear the name of the Most High so that the rest of the world might see him in them. My obedience to God may be the means of leading someone else.

"Thy way was through the sea, thy path through the great waters; yet thy footprints were unseen. Thou didst lead thy people like a flock by the hand of Moses and Aaron."[30] There are always the invisible ways (who can see a path through the water?), but there are the visible ways, such as these two human beings. "He chose David his servant, and took him from the sheepfolds; from tending the ewes that had young he brought him to be the shepherd of Jacob his people, of Israel his inheritance. With upright heart he tended them, and guided them with skillful hand."[31] Those skillful hands were human hands, hands that had learned to do a human job. God used them to do a harder job, but not one unrelated to what they were accustomed to. This brings us to what may well be another indication of God's will.

Gifts and Abilities

David's experience had prepared him, in heart and in hands, to do the thing God chose him for. When I am looking for the right direction, I ought to take into account what experience I have had, what gifts or propensities are mine, and what the direction of my life heretofore seems to have prepared me for.

"What is that in your hand?" the Lord said to Moses. Moses was objecting to the heavy responsibility God was laying on his shoulders and hoped he might get out of it by pointing to the uselessness of speaking to people who were not going to believe him. The thing he had in his hand at the moment, which happened to be a rod, was the thing God made use of to work a miracle. It turned into a snake. Then God used the hand itself for another miracle.[32]

It is a scriptural principle that the divine energy acts upon the stuff of this world. Jesus had the servants fill the stone jars that happened to be standing there when he made wine from water at the marriage in Cana. He used a boy's lunch, instead of starting from nothing, to feed five thousand people. His own spittle and the dirt at his feet were the remedies for a blind man's eyes.[33] Common things taken into the divine hands accomplished eternal purposes.

The nature of the thing in question is obviously important. Jesus did not use mud and spittle to make wine, or a boy's lunch for a poultice. He does not by any means disregard the sort of person we are when he calls us to do his will. He knows our frame and remembers that we are dust. He knows the weaknesses and strengths, the tastes and fears and prejudices and ignorance and experience of each of us. What he wants to make of us, if we are willing to be made over, is sure to bear a relationship to what we are when we first come to him. It is within his power to transform. It is for us to submit to the transformation.

If we have a narrowly circumscribed view of what constitutes God's work, we will be like the head that says to the foot, "I don't need you." Paul explains the wonderful diversity of the Body of Christ through this vivid analogy of the human body with its varied parts. "God works through different men in different ways, but it is the same God who achieves his purposes through them all."[34]

"Try to have a sane estimate of your capabilities by the light of the faith that God has given to you all."[35]

A particular pattern of what we ourselves expect the will of God to fall into may prevent us from seeing what is quite evident to those outside our situation. We are not always good judges of our own capabilities. Our estimate may be far from sane. "The light of the faith God has given to you all" is important, for in order to see anything by this light, we are required to take our place in the company of other Christians.

I have said earlier that God often isolates a man in order to reveal himself. It is when alone that a man most clearly recognizes God for who he is. But it is in relationship with his fellowmen that he comes to know himself. Seeking the will of God as though it had nothing to do with anybody else leads to all kinds of distortions.

What is in my hand? What is my function in the Body of Christ? Have I something to give? Can I see a place where it is needed now? These questions will help me to know what I ought to do.

Desires

What I like and don't like is a part of my nature. I am only too conscious of this when I am asking God to show me what to do. If I like privacy, he might want me in crowds. If I love the fleshpots of a civilized life, he may ask me to be a pioneer missionary. I hear others talking excitedly about "the things the Lord is doing" in this or that place, and when I search my heart I find it is filled with the hope that he won't do anything like that here.

We can all think of a few things we are afraid of. One thing I have feared ever since I first asked God to accomplish his whole will in my life is my own desires. But I have come to see them in a little different light than I used to. For a long time, I took the view that whatever I might want to do could not possibly be what God wanted me to do. That seemed unarguable. I am a sinner, my desires are sinful, "there is no health in us,"[36] and that's that. I went on the Manichean assumption that I am always and necessarily bent on evil, so it ought to be a relatively simple matter to figure out that the will of God was whatever I didn't want to do. (I heard a man on television say that everything he really wanted was too expensive, too fattening, or illegal.)

A better understanding of Scripture has shown me that even I, chief of miserable offenders that I know myself to be, may now and then actually want what God wants. This is likely to be the case more and more as I practice obedience, but it can also be a very simple and natural thing. "Thou knowest me right well; my frame was not hidden from thee, when I was being made in secret, intricately wrought in the depths of the earth."[37] That frame, spoiled by sin as it is, still has something to do with what God will finally make of me, and if the process of being made into his image has been begun in me by faith, my real wants are becoming more like his.

The psalmist said, "My heart speaketh to me for God."[38] If that heart has been given to God, why shouldn't God use it as his speaker? Even the heart of the king, we are told, is in the hand of the Lord.[39]

"If a pagan asks you to dinner," wrote that severely disciplined saint, Paul, "and you want to go, feel free to eat whatever is set before you."[40] Imagine! "If you want to, if you feel like going, go." That shocked me at first. An invitation to a pagan feast would be the sort of thing I would not have dreamed of accepting without praying long and earnestly. God might want me to go, all right, but not—heaven forbid—because it would be fun. He might want me to go for some exalted reason such as to "witness" to those present (which—heaven help me—would not be fun). So I would have had to inquire very carefully in order to separate my own desires from his. Paul took the whole thing very casually. It could happen any day and, like crossing the street, it might be dangerous. But Paul was writing to Christians, and he assumes that if they went, they went with God. It was nothing to pray and fast over.

There were occasions when Paul attempted to do things he wanted to do but was "prevented by the Holy Spirit."[41] He does not mention

special guidance in the decision to do the thing—it was what he
wanted to do, so he decided to do it—but he certainly had special
guidance to stop, and it came in time, before he strayed off the path
of righteousness. It is, we may properly say, *natural* to trust God to
do this for us once we have made up our minds to follow, and we
need not be forever halting and backing up, paralyzed by fear of our
own desires.

Our human desire is never more powerfully felt than when we
are in love. The experience overwhelmed me, and I did not see how
it would be possible at all to know God's will in such a tempest. John
Greenleaf Whittier's hymn helped me greatly then:

> Breathe through the heats of our desire
>   Thy coolness and Thy balm;
> Let sense be dumb, let flesh retire;
> Speak through the earthquake, wind, and fire,
>   O still, small Voice of calm!

As we have observed so many times in this book, the Lord who
loves us knows how to do this.

Our Own Frame of Reference

God leads me, I believe, within my own frame of reference. What I
am, where I am, how I got there, all have a great deal to do with what
my frame of reference is. God can be counted on to choose the right
avenue of approach.

Consider, for example, the vast differences between the frames of
reference of Rahab, the harlot, David, the handsome young keeper of
sheep, Esther, the loveliest woman in a heathen king's harem, and a tax
collector named Matthew. What of a redheaded monk in Germany,
a noblewoman in the court of Louis XIV, a Russian pilgrim seeking
in the forests and steppes the meaning of the Jesus Prayer, a Bible
Belt farmwife, a Japanese university student, a Jewish psychiatrist, or
a Long Island Episcopalian?

I grew up in a middle-class fundamentalist family in Philadelphia. Family prayers, Sunday school and church, table talk about God and Christian people and Christian work were very much a part of the fabric of my life. It hardly occurred to me that God needed to meet different people in different ways, or that his truth could take forms that would be unrecognizable to me. I saw a certain kind of Christianity in operation, and to me that was what it meant to be a Christian. It took a while for my imagination to go to work to apply that vision to people in other categories such as those listed above, but in the meantime God met me where I was. When I began to learn of the wideness in his mercy, my faith began to grow, and I saw that salvation was a scheme of infinitely vaster dimensions than I had dreamed. And here I had been worrying about whether I would recognize the voice! Rahab heard him, Luther heard him, so did Karl Stern, a Bavarian Jew who tells of his conversion to Christianity in a beautiful book, *Pillar of Fire*.

My frame of reference included, for example, the notion that every decision ought to be confirmed by some specific Scripture verse, gotten in some special way. I prayed for this and often received it. Someone is sure to point out here that it is possible to find a Scripture verse for anything one wants to do ("Let . . . the filthy still be filthy,"[42] for example), so it hardly constitutes the guidance of God in a given instance. I agree. But the experience I am talking about is that of a girl who had set her heart to obey. That has to make a difference. God makes concessions, if I may call them that, to the thing I think I need, if the request is not a presumptuous one.

There are many Christians in the world to whom it would not even occur that God would speak as I thought he did to me, directly. Their frame of reference would include a church and a confessor and spiritual exercises I never heard of. They would expect God to instruct them only through those media. There are those who see visions and dream dreams and listen for the divine call through those. There are some who take the view that they must simply muddle through and hope God will be nice to them.

Whatever our views, they are probably too narrow. Our God is, as J. B. Phillips has said, too small. But the wonderful thing is that God is willing to start there. He can lead us into what the psalmist calls large and even wealthy places.

Circumstances

Once upon a time some donkeys got loose and wandered off from where they were supposed to be. It was this apparently haphazard incident that opened the way for the anointing of the first king of Israel.

"Now the asses of Kish, Saul's father, were lost."[43] The young Saul's having to hunt for them brought him face-to-face with Samuel, the man of God. The timing was perfect—how did the donkeys know when to get lost, how did Saul arrive just as Samuel had come to the city to make a sacrifice (for Saul had nearly turned back home at one point)?—and the man of God had been informed on the previous day what to expect: "Tomorrow about this time I will send to you a man."[44] Saul was not conscious of having been divinely sent. He was only looking for those wretched animals of his father.

Circumstances are without question a part of God's will. "We know that to those who love God, who are called according to his plan, everything that happens fits into a pattern for good."[45] This is a sweeping statement. But if God is in control of the big things, he has to be in control of the little things. He "pulls strings through circumstances," Jim Elliot wrote. It is a normal assumption of faith that he will use circumstances to nudge me in the right direction.

But we have to use our heads. I hope that, in studying the divine principles, we have not forgotten the importance of the human principle of common sense. The intelligence we have is a gift from God; the circumstances in which we find ourselves he controls. Obviously we have to bring our intelligence as well as our faith to bear on those circumstances.

"I will instruct you and teach you the way you should go; I will counsel you with my eye upon you. Be not like a horse or a mule, without understanding, which must be curbed with bit and bridle."[46]

It is possible to become quite mulish in our stubborn insistence on a particular means of guidance so that we miss entirely the signs that are all around us. If we are "without understanding," God may have to impose some uncomfortable "bit" or "bridle" to bring us into line. How much more pleasant things are for all of us, if we will only use our heads.

If a pipe bursts, even the most pious among us is unlikely to drop to his knees to pray about calling the plumber. He calls the plumber first. Any praying can be done later. But in situations that, for particular personal reasons have become highly charged with the idea of "the will of God," the action to be taken may be just as obvious as calling the plumber, but we hesitate to take it. "Lean not unto thine own understanding," we read in Proverbs.[47] Might it not be a kind of worldliness to follow common sense? The first clause of the verse is, "Trust in the LORD with all thine heart," which is a Hebrew parallelism, another way of saying, "Lean not unto thine own understanding." They come to the same thing. A full trust protects us from our own misconceptions.

I knew a girl in college who looked on circumstances as nothing more than the devil's pitfalls. She felt she had to inquire of God before making her bed or helping her roommate with the cleaning. Once she had to borrow shampoo because, halfway to town to buy some, she received a divine directive to go back. This kind of piety is hard to live with, to say the least.

Our Lord himself, when he was on earth, took note of circumstances when he made decisions. He was no automaton, although he always did the things that pleased the Father. The Gospel accounts come to us quite unequivocally as human stories. We see in them Jesus the Man, the Son of man, walking, as we are meant to walk, by faith. Prophecy was fulfilled in what he did, but we cannot assume that he deliberately made decisions in order to fulfill it. "Now when he heard that John had been arrested, he withdrew into Galilee; and leaving Nazareth he went and dwelt in Capernaum by the sea, in the territory of Zebulun and Naphtali, that what was spoken by the prophet Isaiah might be fulfilled."[48] It was not until he *heard* that John had been arrested that he went to Galilee. The arrest was news to him. The news affected his plans. And what he did turned out to be, as Matthew wrote about it later, a fulfillment of Old Testament prophecy.

"Seeing the crowds, he went up on the mountain, and when he sat down his disciples came to him. And he opened his mouth and taught them. . . ."[49] Because of the great things he had done in Syria, the crowds came, and because the crowds came, he gave them that matchless sermon, a treasury of teaching preserved for us today as the Sermon on the Mount. One circumstance leads to another and another, and so God gives us his gifts.

When the disciples asked where Jesus wanted to eat the Passover, his directions included a man going about his ordinary business. Wouldn't it have been just as easy, we may ask, for Jesus to have given directions straight to the house? But he chose to include a man who at that crucial moment would be carrying a water jar. The disciples were to follow him. He must have been a servant, for the house he went to was not his own. A householder also became part of the plot when the disciples had to ask him for the use of his room.[50] These details are so matter-of-factly included that we hardly notice them until we go back over the story and ponder the fact that these were Jesus' specific instructions. His divine knowledge acted on everyday circumstances—it did not bypass them.

When Abraham sent his servant back to his own country to find a wife for his son Isaac, the servant had misgivings as to whether he could accomplish so delicate a mission. Abraham reassured him. It would work because God had promised to give the land of Canaan to Abraham's own descendants, and therefore God would send an angel to help him. (Having had several encounters with angels himself, Abraham assumed that this was the most likely means God would use to direct the servant.)

No angel appears in the story at all. The servant, in fact, set out on his errand in a thoroughly businesslike fashion, packing up ten camel-loads of presents. Nothing is said of his pausing for prayer until he came to the outskirts of the city of Nahor, where he stopped the camel train near the well and prayed for guidance. But his prayer was not one I would have thought of. Instead of asking God to point out to him, from among the women who would soon be coming to draw water, the one he had in mind for Isaac, he asked that the one he *himself* should pick might be the one.

It was an original and imaginative way of ascertaining the will of God. The servant, a man of faith like his master, was not bogged down with preconceived notions of how to ask and how not to ask. His prayer fit his own frame of reference quite well.

The first girl who came was a beautiful one, a virgin, a willing worker, and gracious. When the servant asked her for a drink she quickly let the jar down from her head onto her hand, gave him a drink, and then rushed back to draw water for all of his ten camels. (I have no idea how many jarfuls those beasts must have guzzled, but I am sure it meant a lot of hard work for the girl.) No wonder the servant suspected she was the one, but he had good sense and the patience of faith. "The man gazed at her in silence to learn whether the LORD had prospered his journey or not."[51]

When it turned out that she was indeed a descendant of the city father himself, and that the servant would be welcome in her father Bethuel's house, the servant had his answer. His response was worship: "Blessed be the LORD, the God of my master Abraham, who has not forsaken his steadfast love and his faithfulness toward my master. As for me, the LORD has led me in the way to the house of my master's kinsmen."[52] The King James Version says, "I being in the way, the LORD led me."

No angel, no vision, no word was given. The man was doing his duty, using his head, keeping his eyes open, and trusting in the Lord.

There is no way for us mortals to sort out which of the events in the story of Abraham's servant, or in our own story, are "providential," which really mattered, and which did not. We accept by faith that all of them matter. If we try to trace what look to us like the significant events or turning points in any life, we will not go far before we find it was in the ordinary course that the extraordinary happened. It was where the man with the water jar went (and he went quite naturally and innocently, unaware of being followed or guided) that the Lord wanted his disciples to go. So it is that when we are least aware, goodness and mercy are still following us.

Advice from Friends

It is a good thing to talk over a decision with a friend. The times we find ourselves entirely alone in the making of a decision are rare. Nearly always there are others who will be affected by what we decide, and usually some of these can be consulted. A person who loves God and has had some experience in finding his will is the kind we should look for. I have been very lucky or, to use an old word that means the same thing, blessed, in having several friends of my own age who have helped me often. But I have been especially blessed through the advice of men and women much older than I. They see things I simply don't see. They've been over roads I've never traveled. They have perspective I couldn't possibly have.

> E'en down to old age all My people shall prove
> My boundless, eternal, unchangeable love.[53]

Of course they are better equipped to know that love—they have seen it in operation much longer and in many more ways than I have.

It may be that you cannot find anyone who can advise you, but you can find someone who will pray with you. "If two of you agree on earth about anything they ask, it will be done for them by my Father in heaven."[54] I have seen this work. There is a special power in the union and communion of two or more agreed on asking for a single specific thing.

After Jesus had gone back up to heaven and the disciples were left alone for the first time on their own, a decision had to be made as to who would take the place of the traitor Judas in the ministry of the apostles. Peter brought the matter to the attention of the believers who had gathered for prayer. Before they started praying, they nominated two. Then they prayed, "Lord, who knowest the hearts of all men, show which one of these two thou hast chosen. . . ."[55] They took it "by faith." They assumed that God was in the choice of the nominees to begin with. Now all that remained was for him to make clear which one it should be. They had exercised their responsibility. They expected him to exercise his. They did not look for a shaft of light to strike the right man or a halo to appear around his head. They resorted to the method any man in the street would have thought of: they cast lots. (We would be more likely to cast votes today, but would we as readily accept the winner as God's choice?) The lot fell on Matthias, and he was enrolled with the other eleven. The whole process strikes me as orderly and sensible, which is what I would expect God's way to be.

It is natural to ask advice. It is also natural that friends whose advice we have not asked may offer advice because they genuinely care about our welfare. As Christians, members one of another, subject to one another, we cannot blithely ignore the carefully considered counsel of our friends.

But then they may be wrong, In Acts 20 and 21 we find the story of Paul on his way to Jerusalem. He had resolved, we learn in chapter 19, *in the Spirit*, to go to Jerusalem. He was fully aware of how dangerous this might be for him, and the riot he caused in Ephesus would have been enough to discourage a man of lesser determination. But he had made up his mind, and in the first part of the twentieth chapter the words "determined," "he had arranged," "intending," "Paul had decided," and "he was hastening to be at Jerusalem" make it clear how thoroughly he had decided. He said, "I am going to Jerusalem bound in the Spirit." His own safety was not a consideration. He was interested in one thing: "if only I may accomplish my course and the ministry which I received from the Lord Jesus, to testify to the gospel of the grace of God."[56]

When Paul stopped at Tyre, the Christians in that city were alarmed to learn where he was going, and "through the Spirit they told Paul not to go on to Jerusalem."[57] His resolve to go there had been made "in the Spirit." The Christians' warning not to go was also made through that same Spirit. It looks like a strange contradiction.

This story came to my attention when I, too, had made the decision I referred to earlier as one of my most difficult. It alarmed some who were closest to me and whose opinions I respected. There had been a long period of prayer and preparation for this move, and when it seemed that the time had come, I wrote to my family and a few close friends about it, not actually asking their advice but simply stating my intention. Their response was immediate and almost unanimous: Please don't go. Of course I was confused by this. Was I to conclude that my own leading had been mistaken? Should I take their advice? Could God possibly have shown me one way and them another?

God could have. I found that the two things might both be included in his plan. The warnings of friends were a test of the validity of my call. I was forced to sit down again, weigh all the evidence, count the cost, note the risks, and take them all to God in prayer. He knew my side of the question; he knew their side as well. Like Hezekiah, I spread the letters of my friends before him and waited for some further word. I knew I could not act without regard for others. My awareness of God's will for me, far from making me deaf to godly advice, made me listen the more carefully and wait with greater patience and quietness for the final signal. (This, I might add, was no easy matter for me. I felt as though I were being held in with bit and bridle, and I champed.) But at last the signal was given. An approach to the Auca tribe was suddenly opened to me.

Paul continued his journey despite the advice of the Christians in Tyre. When he got to Caesarea, a prophet named Agabus told him quite plainly that he would be imprisoned in Jerusalem. Shouldn't Paul have taken this as God's message that he ought to change his plans?

His traveling companions and the Caesarean Christians, hearing the prophecy, begged him not to go on. But Paul rebuked them for crying and breaking his heart. He was ready for prison if it came to that, even for death, and his orders were clear. When the Christians saw that nothing would change his mind they stopped crying and said, "The will of the Lord be done." So to Jerusalem Paul went and was arrested as predicted.

We can hardly help speculating as to what might have happened if he had heeded the warnings. We may wonder if Paul was in fact mistaken, and those who warned him were really the voice of God, which he ignored. (Questions like this came to my mind, naturally, when my husband was killed doing what he thought God had called him to do.) We only know it was to Paul's own master he had to answer, and it was Paul who wrote of that wonderful "pattern for good" toward which all things work when we love God. What we know of Paul would convince us he acted in faith, and what we know of God helps us to believe that verse. *Everything* works for good. Those who had warned him might well have said, "We told you so," but their faith may later have enabled them to believe that even his imprisonment would work for good.

It is not, however, as though God allows us to see what may look to us like "good reasons" for his letting things turn out as they did. Sometimes, of course, he does. But we must beware of insisting on some "justification" or vindication that satisfies *us*. God has never promised any such vindication here in this life. He is under no obligation whatever to explain himself. He did not answer Job's questions. He does not answer all of ours. It is faith and faith alone that can believe things fit into a pattern for good. The human evidence points in the other direction.

For some, the death of five men at the hands of Auca Indians was "justified" by the salvation of some of the Aucas. What could we say, then, of the thousands of Indians (the Aucas numbered only a few hundred) in the tribes with whom the men had been working before their attempt to reach the Auca tribe? Such attempts to figure out why things happen, to allay our own fears and shore up our crumbling defenses, are not the response of faith. Where reasons are given, we don't need faith. Where only darkness surrounds us, we have no means for seeing except by faith.

There was no human explanation offered me for my husband's death that adequately covered the data. Nothing satisfied me except the absolute conviction that God was in perfect control. It did not look as though he was. It looked like chaos. Faith alone enabled me to believe in that pattern for good.

There was a time when Paul had no advice from anybody. After (we are not told how long after) his stunning conversion on the road to Damascus, "I did not confer with flesh and blood, nor did I go up to Jerusalem to those who were apostles before me" (I am surprised that he felt no need to consult even men qualified as apostles), "but I went away into Arabia."[58] Not a word is written of what he did there. We only know that he had no conferences with anybody.

But Paul was a special case. He had special experiences (his conversion, his calling), he did some special things in special ways, and most of us would assume from the start that we cannot imitate him. He went up to Jerusalem "by revelation." He does not explain what this means, but it must have been something special.

Let us not forget, however, that to God each of us is a special case. There is no category labeled "Miscellaneous." The God who guided the great apostle in his great work is the God who carries lambs in his arms.

> If thou but suffer God to guide thee,
>   And hope in Him through all thy ways,
> He'll do thee good, whate'er betide thee,
>   And bear thee through the evil days.
> Who trusts in God's unchanging love
> Builds on the Rock that naught can move.
>
> Georg Neumark
> (tr. Catherine Winkworth)

The Harder of Two Things

Sometimes we have narrowed down the possibilities to two, but there seems no way to choose one of them. "How long will you go limping with two different opinions?" Elijah asked the people of Israel. "If the LORD is God, follow him; but if Baal, then follow him."[59] The people had been thrown into confusion by Ahab the king, and Elijah was sent to straighten them out. It was a question as to which god was the true one. Clearly it had to be one or the other. Elijah the prophet and truth-teller was not really welcome, for he would clarify the issues and force the people to a choice.

But such clarification and pressure is exactly what is needed where there is confusion, and it is exactly what the word of God does. It strips away whatever is irrelevant and dispenses with the side issues, "piercing to the division of soul and spirit, of joints and marrow, and discerning the thoughts and intentions of the heart. And before him no creature is hidden, but all are open and laid bare to the eyes of him with whom we have to do."[60]

Most of us avoid crises when we can. It is far more comfortable to sit in the back row than to stand up and be counted. It is less demanding to fade into the crowd, stay in the shade, move at our accustomed pace. To take up the cross and follow, to walk in the light, to climb "the steep ascent of heaven"[61] are not options that have a strong popular appeal.

But we are speaking of those who actually want to do the will of God. What we are concerned with now is the business of choice when both alternatives seem equally moral.

Choose the harder of the two ways. If you have eliminated all other possibilities and there still seem to be two that might please God, choose the more difficult one. "The way is hard, that leads to life,"[62] Jesus said, so it is likely that he is asking us to will against our will.

But what if he isn't asking that? The more sincerely we seek the will of God, the more fearful we will be that we may miss it. If it made little difference to us, obviously we would not worry very much about it, so there ought to be a measure of reassurance for us in the very fact of our fear. Jesus is in the boat with us, no matter how wild the storm is, and he is at peace. He commands us not to be afraid.

The supreme example outside that of our Lord himself, of a man willing against his own will, in obedience to God, is Abraham. He was asked to sacrifice Isaac, his only son—and this, in the face of all God's promises about descendants. Abraham was to tie the boy down on top of a pile of kindling on an altar. This he did (with what anguish we can only imagine), and only then, when with the knife poised he had triumphantly passed the hardest test of faith, did God show him that his son's death was not finally required.[63]

David was willing to undertake a staggering project, the building of a temple for God. God did not allow him to build it but was pleased with him for wanting to. "You did well that it was in your heart,"[64] God told him.

When Paul, Silas, and Timothy were traveling together as missionaries in Asia Minor, "they attempted to go into Bithynia, but the Spirit of Jesus did not allow them."[65] We could wish Luke had told us exactly how the Spirit of Jesus stopped them, but it is enough for us to know that the men who were bent on obedience to God had made, in the integrity of their hearts (we may believe), a wrong decision and that God reversed it.

"And your ears shall hear a word behind you, saying, 'This is the way, walk in it,' when you turn to the right or when you turn to the left."[66]

study guide

study one: the model prayer

study two: what is promised

study three: the conditions: part one

study four: the conditions: part two

study five: the objectives

study six: the supernatural means

study seven: the natural means

the model prayer

Read: Matthew 6:9–15

A thoughtful consideration of the words of the Lord's Prayer will help us to put our minds in the right frame before we begin knocking on God's door for guidance in some particular matter. This is the model prayer Jesus gave his disciples when they asked him to teach them to pray. It is all-inclusive and therefore furnishes the context for all prayers, including, "Lead me, Lord. Show me what to do."

The Lord's Prayer contains an address, a description, and six petitions.

The Address: Our Father

Key thought: If we trust the Son who died for us and come to the Father aware of our need of his grace, we may take our position before him as a child, not knowing what is best for us but coming and asking to be shown what to do. It is merely a request, not a demand, and can be granted or refused. Surely any father would look tenderly on a child's desire to be shown what to do. Certainly God will show us.

1. Study Matthew 7:7–11. What does this passage tell you about God's desire for you? *He wants me to have all I need and give me an abundance*

2. Read James 1:17. What does this mean? _Everything_
   we have is from God

3. How is God similar to an earthly father? _____
   _____
   _____
   _____

   How is he different? _____
   _____
   _____
   _____

The Description: Who Art in Heaven

Key thought: Our heavenly Father knows every inch of our earthly journey, sees it whole, and has been over the course himself.

1. What does Psalm 115:3 tell you about God? _____
   He does what makes him
   happy

2. Study Psalm 139:13–16. What does this passage say about the manner in which God plans your life? _He has_
   always known the plans for
   my life, the choices I will
   make and how it ends.

   How does this make you more confident of God's guidance?
   _____
   _____
   _____
   _____

(margin, vertical handwriting): Who will get credit if God answers my prayers?

The First Petition: Hallowed Be Thy Name

Key thought: God longs for his children to be actively involved with him through prayer. Because he loves us, he gives us a part to play in hallowing his name here on earth.

1. What does it mean to hallow? _____
   _____
   _____
   _____
   _____

2. What are some ways in which you can hallow God's name here on earth? _____
   _____
   _____
   _____

3. According to John 4:23–24, how are you to worship God?_____
   _____in the Spirit and in truth._____
   _____
   _____
   _____
   _____

4. In what ways can you worship God in spirit and in truth?_____
   _____
   _____
   _____

The Second Petition: Thy Kingdom Come

Key thought: As you lay your individual prayers before God, you do so recognizing that the answer has to fit into the coming of the kingdom and the holiness of the name.

1. Ephesians 1:20–23 describes the nature of the kingdom of Christ. What are some of the characteristics of this kingdom? _____
   It is the most powerful and
   everything will bow to him.
   _____

2. A king rules over his subjects. In what ways does God rule over you? _____
   _____
   _____

The Third Petition: Thy Will Be Done on Earth As It Is in Heaven

Key thought: Jesus teaches us to pray for the coming of the kingdom in the only way the kingdom can possibly come: through the doing of the Father's will. As we learn to live more intimately with him, it will become our sole object in life. In every act that accords with his will, we are also hallowing his name.

1. How would you define God's will? _____
   _____
   _____
   _____

2. Read the account of Jesus praying in Gethsemane (Matt. 26:36–42). What does this tell you about the importance of doing God's will? _It's okay to be scared of_
   it. It must be done at all
   costs.

3. According to Romans 12:2, how do you determine the will of God? _____
   _____
   _____

4. What are some ways in which God is leading you to do his will in your life? _____

_____

_____

_____

_____

The Fourth Petition: Give Us This Day Our Daily Bread

Key thought: The humble business of ordinary food and ordinary necessities reminds us of our utter dependence on God. To him nothing is trivial or important, nothing small or great, for he is all and fills all in all.

1. Study Matthew 6:25–34. How does trusting in God for your daily bread allow you to seek his kingdom more than anything else?
   You become less consumed by possession and status and begin to have more focus for Him.

2. If God is concerned about everything in your life, when can you ask him for guidance? *Any time in all things.*

3. List some things for which you sometimes forget to seek God's guidance. *Weight loss/food, Chad's activities and future, working vs. not working*

The Fifth Petition: Forgive Us Our Trespasses As We Forgive Those Who Trespass against Us

Key thought: God must often delay the answer to our prayers for special guidance because we have already chosen a path of disobedience. When this happens, we must repent, which means to turn around. Go back to the point of departure. Then pray to be shown the path of God's will.

1. What is a trespass? _____
   _____
   _____
   _____
   _____

2. Read Matthew 18:21–35. What does this passage say about the importance of forgiving others? _____
   We have no right not to forgive.
   _____
   _____

   What will happen if you don't forgive others their trespasses?
   He'll deal with you how you deal with others.
   _____
   _____

3. Can you expect to receive God's guidance if you don't forgive others? _____
   _____
   _____
   _____
   _____

4. Sometimes the fifth petition of the Lord's Prayer is stated as "Forgive us our debts, as we forgive our debtors." How is debt an appropriate description of sin against God and other human beings?

_____

_____

_____

Sixth Petition: Lead Us Not into Temptation but Deliver Us from Evil

Key thought: Temptation is not in itself a sin. Satan uses it to cause us to sin. God's purpose in allowing it is to test our faith, and his Word even tells us to *welcome* it (James 1:2–3).

1. What does 1 Corinthians 10:13 say about temptation? _____
   We should expect it, not feel
   sorry for ourselves, look for
   God's way out.

_____

What does James 1:12–15 say? _temptation_
stems from our own evil
desires, and once we give
in it leads to death

_____

2. Why is God's guidance especially important when you are undergoing temptation? He will help us to
   not want what we want.

_____

_____

_____

Applying God's Truth to Your Life

1. Describe a situation in which you did not seek God's guidance in your life. What was the end result? _____

   _____

   _____

   _____

   _____

2. List three areas of your life in which you would like to seek God's guidance more consistently.

   a. _My Children_____

   b. _My work_____

   c. _My health_____

3. What is the most important lesson that you have learned from this study of the model prayer? _____

   We cannot ask for Guidance

   when we are in the middle

   of our own sin.

   _____

To Do This Week

Commit to praying the Lord's Prayer as a prayer for God's guidance in your life. Each day focus on one of the petitions of this prayer and ask the Lord to show you how that petition can be applied to a specific problem or challenge you are facing.

STUDY TWO

what is promised

Read: Psalm 23

The picture of the Eastern shepherd with his robes and staff, the flock of sheep, the stony path through the ravine, the dark valley, and the grassy place with the quiet pool are so remote from our lives as to seem no more than a romantic painting from another country and another age. We live in towns and cities and suburbs. Our days are full of perplexities far removed from the things that bother rams and ewes and lambs. We muddle along through the thousand decisions of an ordinary day. Some are trivial. Others are important. A student has to decide where to go to college, what to major in, whom to marry, what job to prepare for, where to find that job. After college he or she must decide where to live, how to pay for the house, the car, the furniture, the things that seem so much more indispensable than green pastures.

Is it reasonable to expect today the guidance of the God of the pastures of ancient Israel? Has he ever made any promises that I can get hold of? Is there anything that applies to my needs this Tuesday? Are the promises relevant?

The Wrong Approach

Key thought: Sometimes we come to God confident and, we think, well-informed and well-equipped. We know what we need—a yes or no answer, please, to a simple question. Or perhaps a road sign.

Something quick and easy to point the way. What we really ought to have is the Guide himself—someone who has been there before and knows the way.

1. Read the story of the two young Americans on pages 25–26. What was wrong with their approach? _____

   _____

   _____

   _____

2. Describe an occasion when you took the wrong approach to seeking God's guidance. What happened as a result? _____

   _____

   _____

   _____

The Bible Is Relevant

Key thought: The Bible is relevant—more relevant, more accurate, more trustworthy, more totally applicable to my "case" as a human being than anything a person, no matter how well-trained, can tell me. It is the place to begin. It is the foundation, the only sure one.

1. Read 2 Timothy 3:16. What does Paul mean when he says that all Scripture is inspired or God-breathed? _____

   _____

   _____

   In what four ways is Scripture profitable, according to Paul?

   a. _teaching_____

   b. _correcting_____

   c. _rebuking_____

   d. _training in righteous_____

How does each of these ways teach us that the Bible is a trustworthy guide?

a. _____

b. _____

c. _____

d. _____

2. C. S. Lewis said, "All that is not eternal is eternally out of date." Apply this comment to a situation in your life. _____
_____
_____

The Valley of the Shadow of Death

Key thought: If we actually experience the valley of the shadow, everything but the Living Word of God may then look utterly irrelevant. The question of relevancy at such a time is turned completely over. Perhaps then, for the first time, we know ourselves to be sheep in need of a shepherd. He is our Shepherd. He is there. He hasn't, for a single moment, forgotten his job.

1. Read Psalm 46. To what is God compared? _____
_____
_____

What promises does this psalm make about God in our times of trouble? _____
_____
_____

How does knowing that God is a fortress comfort you? _____
_____
_____
_____

2. God's Word is always relevant. How does it become particularly relevant during times of crisis? _____
_____
_____

3. Describe a recent crisis in your life. How did God's Word help in your time of trouble? _____
_____
_____

The Promises of the Bible

Key thought: The Bible contains thousands of promises, a great number of which concern guidance. Nearly every one of the sixty-six books has some word about how God led someone or how he promises to lead those who want to be led.

1. Read Isaiah 42:16. At times you may feel like a blind person, unable to see the path ahead. What does this passage promise you?
_____
_____
_____

2. At other times you may feel all alone, unsure of yourself and your future. What special promises does Deuteronomy 31:6 provide for you? _No matter what is coming_
you do not have to fear.
_____

3. Are you afraid of failing in an undertaking? Examine Psalm 56:13 and describe its promise of God's guidance. _____
Wife, mother, home caretaker.
_____
_____
_____

4. Perhaps you are undergoing persecution of one sort or another. Read Psalm 3. What does it say about God's ability to deliver you?

_____

_____

_____

5. Are you fatigued, too weary to go on? Exodus 33:14 and Matthew 11:28 contain a special promise for you. What is this promise?

_He will provide you rest_____

_____

_____

A Matter of Trust

Key thought: The Bible contains plenty of evidence that God has guided people. He is willing to guide me. He has been at it for a long time. His hand reaches toward me. I have only to take it.

1. Read the story of the travels along the jungle trails of Ecuador on pages 29–30. How is trusting a human guide like trusting in God?

_____

_____

_____

How is it different? _____

_____

_____

_____

2. Proverbs 3:5–6 tells you to trust in the Lord. What will he do for you if you trust in him? _____

_____

_____

_____

Applying God's Truth to Your Life

1. What are your most important daily concerns? How can you more effectively seek God's guidance in dealing with them?_____

   Worshipping the Creator rather than the created. Being honest & effective in all my relationships.

2. Identify some of your long-range goals and describe how trusting in God's guidance will help you shape those goals._____

   My weight –
   Paying off debt –

3. Review Psalm 23. List three ways in which the promises of this psalm assure you of God's guidance in your life.

   a. _____

   b. _____

   c. _____

To Do This Week

Read Psalm 23 every day. Take one verse each day and ask the Lord to show you how the promises of that verse apply to a specific situation in your life. Pray that the Lord will give you the courage to trust in his guidance in that situation.

The Beloved Unbeliever
Ernesto

STUDY THREE

the conditions: part one

Read: Exodus 3

God's promises to guide cover every imaginable situation. All we need to do is take the hand he stretches out. But it is here that the hardest question arises: How, exactly, do I take his hand?

He has said over and over, "I will guide you." But there are so many promises with conditions attached, conditions that seem impossible to fulfill. The promises *seem* to say, "I will give you the light you are asking for *if* . . ." When I read what follows the "if," I find that a great deal is asked of me in exchange. Who does God think I am, that I can meet such demands before he will answer my prayer?

What are the conditions God attaches to the promises of his guidance? There are several.

The Recognition of Who God Is

Key thought: The best kind of beginning, when we are wanting to know the will of God, is to concentrate first on God himself. The briefest effort to do this will humble us.

1. Read Isaiah 43:14–15. Who is God according to this passage?

   <u>Redeemer, Holy One, Creator, King</u>

   _____

   _____

How does knowing that God is your Redeemer help you trust in his guidance? _he didn't give up on Israel he won't give up on me._

How does knowing that God is your King help? _____
Does not abuse his authority

2. In Exodus 3:14 God reveals himself to Moses by the name *Yahweh* (the LORD). As Exodus 3 makes clear, Yahweh means "I AM." What does it mean to you that God is the great I AM? _____
He is my past my present and is in my future, I don't need to worry.

3. Immediately after revealing himself to Moses as I AM, God promises to deliver the Israelites from their slavery in Egypt. How does this illustrate the guidance of God? _Everything is intentional, it will all be used by him._
(Stacey's knitting example.)

Belief

Key thought: Faith means believing that God means what he says.

1. God has promised to guide you. Why is faith in this promise a precondition of accepting God's guidance? _____

2. Is it possible to truly believe that God will guide you if you don't have faith? _____ No _____

_____

_____

3. Describe a situation in which lack of faith kept you from accepting God's guidance. _____

_____

_____

_____

The Obedience of Faith

Key thought: Even a casual look at God's Word shows me that a relative goodness won't do. I am none of the things I am told I need to be in order to expect God's guidance. However, what we can't do, Someone has done for us. Jesus is our guide, and he is himself the Way.

1. Read Psalm 25:9–10. Whom has God promised to guide? ____
   ___ the humble and obediant _____

_____

_____

   Does this mean that you have to be good if you expect God to guide you? Why or why not? _we can only_
   "be good" when covered in Jesus's
   righteousness

_____

2. Study Romans 8:9–16. Briefly describe what Paul is saying in this passage. _____

_____

_____

_____

Nothing we can do cancels our sin.

According to this passage, who enables you to obey God? _____
Holy Spirit
_____
_____

How does knowing this fact comfort you and assure you that God
will guide you? _He can overcome_
all things
_____
_____

The Glory of the Name

Key thought: If we did not have God's unequivocal promise, the
words "Guide *me*, for the sake of *your* name" would sound outrageously
presumptuous. But the truth is that God said he would do just this.
There is nothing presumptuous or precarious about it. The validity
of the divine word is at stake, and that is a very sure foundation.

1. Write out Psalm 31:3. _Since you are my_
   rock and my fortress for the sake
   of your name lead and guide me
   _____

   Why does the psalmist appeal to God's name as a reason for asking him to provide guidance? _____
   _____
   _____
   _____

2. One of the names ascribed to God in Isaiah 9:6 is "Wonderful
   Counselor." What is a counselor? _____
   _____
   _____
   _____

How does knowing that God is a wonderful counselor assure you of his guidance? _Because he has shown us proof of what he can do._

Read Isaiah 9:1–7. Who is this Wonderful Counselor? (See Matthew 4:12–16.) _Jesus_

Making a Beginning

Key thought: To believe one thing—this one promise that God will guide us, for example—is a baby step. It is a beginning of a walk with God. The steps that follow will be like the first one in that they contain the element of faith. If God means it this time, he means it the next time. I take him at his word now, and I will hear another word tomorrow.

1. Hebrews 11:1 tells us that "faith is being sure of what we hope for and certain of what we do not see" (NIV). Why is it important to be *sure* and *certain* if you are going to take the steps of faith necessary to walk with God? _Because you may not like where you are going so you need to trust to follow when it gets tough._

2. Think of what it is like to walk somewhere. Why is taking the first step so important? _A deed begun is half done - you will never get anywhere_

Why is it equally important that you don't *just* take the first step? _You may not be the good soil. Maturity can not occur with only one step._

3. The road of life may have varying degrees of difficulty. But the Pioneer has traveled it before us. There will be no ravines he cannot cross. He knows the way; he has been over every foot of it.

How does knowing that Jesus has been over the road assure you that you can trust his guidance? _____
_____
_____

Applying God's Truth to Your Life

1. What obstacles stand in the way of your recognizing that God will provide guidance for your life? _unbelief_
_____
_____

2. Reread Exodus 3. God promised to deliver the Israelites from their slavery in Egypt. From what forms of slavery do you want God to deliver you? _Food, $$, seeking comfort_
from sources other than God
_____

3. What is the most important lesson that you have learned from this study of the conditions for God's guidance? _____
_____
_____
_____

To Do This Week

Each day identify a specific circumstance in your life in which you sense the need for God's guidance. Pray that God will enable you to take the first step in trusting him to guide you in that circumstance.

the conditions: part two

Read: Luke 9:18–27

The taking up of the cross will mean sooner or later saying no to self. But it is also a resounding yes. It means saying yes when everything in us says no, deciding to do the thing that we do not want to do because it is not "natural." And in our giving of wholehearted assent, we find to our amazement that the impossible becomes possible and the things we were sure were beyond us are now within reach, for God's command is his enabling. *Never* has he given an assignment that was not accompanied by the power to accomplish it.

The cross entails sacrifice, too. There is no getting around this. Christianity has been criticized and rejected by many as an "unnatural" religion, a life that denies living, a negation and not an affirmation. Jesus never tried to make it look easy. The principles he taught cut across the grain of human nature: Lose your life in order to find it; be poor in spirit if you want to be happy; mourn if you want to rejoice; take the last place if you want the first. The corn of wheat must first fall into the ground and die if it is ever to produce anything.

What we must not forget is that Jesus traveled this road before us. "He himself endured a cross and thought nothing of its shame"—not because he had a particular liking for self-denial and suffering but "because of the joy he knew would follow his suffering. . . . Think constantly of him enduring all that sinful men could say against him, and you will not lose your purpose or your courage" (Heb. 12:2–3 PHILLIPS).

Prayer

Key thought: Faith requires action. Perhaps the most "natural" activity is prayer. If we know the one in whom we have believed, we turn to him for help. The single kind of help most frequently prayed for in the Bible is guidance.

1. Study Psalm 25. What does it mean for God to guide you in his truth (v. 5 NIV)? _____

    _____

    _____

    _____

    Whose path are we to seek when we pray (v. 4)? _____

    _____

    _____

    _____

    _____

    _____

    Why should we seek God's path? _____

    _____

    _____

    _____

    _____

    Why will God instruct you in his ways (v. 8)? _____

    _____

    _____

    _____

2. The simple bringing of the request to God is an acknowledgment that we need him.

What do you think are the most important requests for you to bring to God in prayer? _Life Changes, Children,_ _Marriage, Intercession, all things_ _big and small_

What factors stand in the way of regularly bringing your requests to God? _____

3. Carefully read Philippians 4:6. In what spirit are you to bring your requests to God? _Should be requests not_ _demands_

If God already knows what you need, why should you bother bringing your requests to God? (See pages 44–45.) _It_ _brings us into fellowship with_ _Him._

According to Philippians 4:6, what wrongful attitude will prayer prevent? Why? _Anxiety, fear, the need to_ _control what is going on_

4. What does Matthew 7:7–12 promise you if you bring your requests to God? _____
_____
_____
_____

Does this mean that God will always answer your prayer the way you want? Why or why not? _____
_____
_____
_____

In what way will God answer prayer, according to Romans 8:26–28? _____
_____
_____
_____

How does this passage in Romans assure you that God will give you what is best for you? *Because the Spirit is interceding for us, and the Spirit is God*
_____
_____

Fasting

Key thought: Fasting is not a good way of getting one's mind off food, but it is a way of deliberately putting one's mind on one thing (God) because you are reminded every minute of the other thing (food). The fact that you have made up your mind not to eat keeps before you the reason you are not eating. You are after something specific from God, and although your own will may be too weak to desire his will, it is at least strong enough for this one small thing. God in his mercy and fatherly love takes note of this flicker of movement toward him.

1. Study Acts 14:23. What were the circumstances in which Paul
   and Barnabas were fasting? *or* They were
   appointing church leaders

   What does this tell you about the value of fasting when facing an
   important decision? _____

2. How should you fast, according to Matthew 6:16–18? _____
   Don't look sad, don't draw
   attention to yourself

   What will be the result of fasting in the right spirit? _____
   He will reward you.
   A changed life.

One Man's Cross

Key thought: The cross is the thing required of me today. "Let him
take up his cross *daily*," Jesus said, "and follow me" (Luke 9:23). Some
duty lies on my doorstep right now. It may be a simple thing I have
known for a long time I ought to do, but it has been easy to avoid. It
is probably the thing that springs to my mind when I pray the prayer,
"We have left undone those things which we ought to have done"
(*Book of Common Prayer*).

1. When people speak of bearing crosses, what sort of burdens are they typically thinking of? _____

   _____

   _____

   _____

   _____

2. It may be that, although I have been doing something I ought to do, I have never done it without grudging. The so-called cross I could not avoid I may, for a change, take up with gladness. Might I not then, for the first time, be on the way to true discipleship?

   List some things you have been doing grudgingly. _____

   _____

   _____

   _____

   How does the idea of taking up your cross allow you to approach these duties in a more cheerful spirit? _____

   _____

   _____

   _____

3. Jesus says that you must "take up [your] cross daily and follow me" (Luke 9:23). In following him, you are treating him as your master. You are obeying him. If you obey him, can you rightly expect his guidance? Why? _____

   _____

   _____

   _____

   If you refuse to obey, can you still expect him to guide? Why not? _____

   _____

   _____

4. The cross entails sacrifice. There is no getting around this. What one thing do you believe God is asking you to sacrifice above all else? _____

_____

_____

_____

Applying God's Truth to Your Life

1. List three of the most important requests for guidance that you wish to bring before God.

   a. _____

   b. _____

   c. _____

2. Have you ever fasted when faced with an important decision? If so, what was the result? _____

_____

_____

_____

3. What cross or crosses do you believe God is asking you to take up today? _____

_____

_____

_____

To Do This Week

Each day pray that God will show you what cross he wants you to take up on that day. If you are facing a crucial decision, try fasting in preparation for making that decision.

the objectives

Read: John 14

Christ is the ultimate objective. Christ himself is also the Way. The things that are promised along the way (his presence, guidance, peace, light, assurance) and the conditions entailed by the promises are inextricably linked to the final object God has in mind.

We want to know the right way. Coming to God, we have come to the right place, for we have come to the One who not only can tell us the way, show us the truth, and give us life but who also has said, "I am the way, the truth, and the life" (John 14:6). Jesus identifies himself here in one of his great *I am* statements, and we are reminded of the primary condition of asking for help: the recognition of who God is. He is everything we are asking for. He is the Alpha, for nothing would have begun without him. He is the Omega, for it is in him that everything finds its perfection and fulfillment. These are mysteries that go deeper than we can fathom, but there are simpler terms which may help us.

The Father's House

Key thought: The Father's house is where we belong, and the way to it, as in the story of the prodigal son, is repentance. Christ leads us to the first objective.

1. Read the parable of the prodigal son (Luke 15:11–32). Why was repentance necessary before this son could return to his father?

   _____

   _____

   _____

   Why is it necessary for you to repent if you are to come home to your heavenly Father? _____

   _____

   _____

   _____

2. The Greek word for repentance is *metanoia*, which literally means "a changing of one's mind." In what ways is repentance like a change of mind? _____

   _____

   _____

   _____

3. God also calls you to be holy, or sanctified. Write out 1 Peter 1:14–16. _____

   _____

   _____

   _____

   Why does Peter link the idea of holiness to obedience? _____

   _____

   _____

   _____

   Into what sort of life should you expect God's guidance to lead you? _____

   _____

   _____

   _____

His Name's Sake

Key thought: God is not primarily concerned about our reputations. We ought to be willing to allow God to do "special" things for us and to accept them quietly, confident that whatever he does fits into the working out of his purposes for us all.

1. According to Psalm 106:7–10, why did the Lord save the Israelites by taking them through the Red Sea? _____

   _____

   _____

   _____

   _____

   _____

   What does this tell you about the reason God protects you from danger and from enemies? _____

   _____

   _____

   _____

   _____

2. Read Psalm 23:3. According to this verse, why will God guide you? _____

   _____

   _____

   _____

   What does it mean for God to do something for his name's sake? _____

   _____

   _____

   _____

3. If you are going through a time of trouble, why can you expect
   God to deliver you, according to Psalm 143:11? _____

   _____

   _____

   _____

4. If God guides you for his name's sake, who is glorified whenever
   your prayers for guidance are answered? _____

   _____

   _____

   _____

Help for Others

Key thought: God gives to us in order that we may give to others.
Whatever he does in the course of our lives, he gives us, through the
experience, some power to help others.

1. Matthew 10:8 says in part, "Freely you have received, freely give."
   What are the most important things you have received from God?

   _____

   _____

   _____

   How can you use these things to help others? _____

   _____

   _____

   _____

2. We need to remember that if we are asking for something that will
   end with us or shut us off from others, a dead-end kind of thing
   we have prayed for without much regard for our responsibility to
   other people, it may be withheld.

What are some selfish prayers that people pray? _____
_____
_____
_____

If you pray without regard for your responsibility to others, how might God choose to answer your prayers? _____
_____
_____
_____

Commitment

Key thought: The initial choice to go the whole way with God is made of necessity in ignorance of all that will follow. We have been warned that the road will be a hard one, for our Master himself walked a hard road.

1. Read the illustration of riding a roller coaster on page 59. How is this an apt illustration of your commitment to God? _____
_____
_____
_____

2. Study Luke 9:57–62. What does this passage say about the importance of total commitment to the Lord? _It is all_
or nothing
Is Christ your whole life with everything
fitting into him? Or are you trying to
fit Christ into your life?
What excuses do people use to avoid this sort of commitment?
_____
_____
_____

What excuses have you used? *I have to many things to do, I do more than others do, I have things to do first then I'll ...*

3. Commitment often results in suffering. How does Romans 8:17–18 comfort you when commitment to Christ leads to suffering? *that we are heirs suffering as he suffered.*

Thanksgiving

Key thought: It is even possible to be thankful for the valley of the shadow, not because we like it or find anything to enjoy in that fearsome ravine but because we have been told ahead of time that it is not the end of the journey. It is on the way to the Lord's house, and when we get there we'll know it was worth enduring any trouble along the way.

1. Study 1 Thessalonians 5:16–18. What three things does this passage tell you to do?
   a. *Rejoice*
   b. *Pray*
   c. *Give thanks*

Why is prayer necessary if you are to follow the commands to be joyful and give thanks? *Prayer reminds us of who we are and what we have to be joyful or thankful for.*

2. How does knowing that God will lead you to your heavenly home allow you to give thanks in times of adversity? _____

_____

_____

_____

_____

The Knowledge of Truth

Key thought: The leading of God toward the full light of truth is, like our recognition of him, a lifelong process, and for this we can be thankful. We move one step at a time, and Christ is the Way and the Truth. He does not drop the whole block of truth into our laps at once, for we could not possibly bear the weight of it.

1. Carefully study John 8:31–32. What is necessary before you can know the truth? _Belief in Jesus_

_____

_____

_____

2. What does 1 John 2:3 say about how you can be assured that you know Jesus? _You keep his commands_

_____

_____

_____

3. It will help us do what we have to do today if we can remember why we do it, especially if it seems to us that the answer we get when we pray for the will of God is beyond our powers. It is then that we need to look beyond our powers, beyond ourselves, beyond our own immediate desires. Let us go over again in our minds God's objectives, and we may be surprised at the ease with which we can then obey.

How does knowing that God is in control of your life enable you to do all things joyfully, even the most humdrum things of life?

to know he has never forgotten me and that nothing is unintentional

Applying God's Truth to Your Life

1. God requires repentance before you can have a right relationship with him. How has repentance helped you have a closer walk with God? _____

_____

_____

2. List three specific areas of your life where you would like to become more obedient to God.

   a. _Honesty in everything_
   b. _submission to my husband_
   c. _Daily time listening, talking, reading_

3. Describe an occasion when you experienced God's guidance through adversity. How did this experience draw you closer to him? ____

_____

_____

_____

To Do This Week

List seven specific events in your life for which you can thank God. Include in this list adversities or difficulties that you are experiencing at present. Each day take one of these items and praise God for it.

the supernatural means

Read: Daniel 2

When God guided by means of the pillar of cloud and fire, by the star of Bethlehem, by visitations of angels, by the word coming through visions and dreams and prophets and even through an insulted donkey, in most cases these were not signs that had been asked for. And when they were asked for, as in the case of Jehoshaphat and Ahab, they were not accepted.

Supernatural phenomena were given at the discretion of the divine wisdom. It is not for us to ask that God guide us in some miraculous way. If, in his wisdom, he knows that such means are what we need, he will surely give them.

Visible Signs

Key thought: If we are ever tempted to wonder whether God can possibly communicate with people who seem to us remote and unlikely prospects, if we doubt his ability to choose a method to suit the individuals involved, if we think of world events as rather haphazard and of specific points in time and space as hardly worth his notice, it will do us good to remember those mysterious strangers and that star.

1. The Bible provides two important examples of visible signs that helped guide the people of God. One is described in Exodus 13:21

and 40:36–37. Another is described in Matthew 2:9–10. What were these signs? _Pillar of fire, cloud_

Matt. Star

How did each sign specifically guide the people for whom it was intended to their destination? _Everyone could see it, it provided shelter_

2. Do you believe that God can still use visible signs if he so chooses? Why or why not? _Yes - He is God_

3. Why do you suppose that such signs were rarely used, even in Bible times? _the awe factor_

Audible Signs

Key thought: There are many occasions recorded in the Bible when "the word of the Lord came"—a voice, clearly heard, clearly understood, clearly identified.

1. Study 1 Kings 17:1–6. This passage records an instance when the word of the Lord came to Elijah. What specific guidance did God give Elijah? _____

Did God fulfill his promise to Elijah? _____

_____

_____

What benefits did Elijah receive by listening to the word of the Lord? _____

_____

_____

2. Later, the Lord provided Elijah with further audible guidance. According to 1 Kings 17:8–9, what did God say to Elijah?
   Get up & Go to a widow

_____

_____

Did Elijah obey (v. 10)? ___Yes he did_____

_____

_____

_____

What were the results of Elijah's obedience to this divine guidance (vv. 10–16)? _____

_____

_____

_____

Angels

Key thought: A study of both the visible and the audible manifestations of angels in the stories of the Bible will probably surprise most of us, for they are not as rare as we usually think of them. However, they came quite unexpectedly (it was not that the man or woman to whom they came had been praying for a supernatural visitor, or even for guidance), and the message they brought was often a startling one.

1. The first time an angel appeared to a human being, according to the biblical record, it was to an outcast Egyptian servant woman, Hagar. This event is recorded in Genesis 16. Why was Hagar running away from her home? *Her mistress was persecuting her*

   What guidance did the angel give Hagar? *Go Home*

   Who was Hagar's son? *Ishmael*

2. Genesis 19 records the appearance of two angels to Lot, Abraham's nephew. Was Lot aware at first that they were angels? _____

   What does this tell you about their appearance? _____

   Why was Lot so hesitant to follow their urgent instructions?

3. In Judges 13 an angel appears to the parents of Samson. What instructions did this angel give Samson's parents concerning their son? _____

_____

_____

_____

How did Manoah, Samson's father, realize that this man was an angel (vv. 6, 20, 21)? _____

_____

_____

_____

Compare the appearance of angels to Lot with their appearance to Manoah and his wife. _____

_____

_____

_____

4. Read Hebrews 13:2. What does this say about man's ability to recognize angels? _____

_____

_____

_____

_____

What does the author of Hebrews believe the visits of angels should teach us concerning hospitality? Always be ready to show hospitality to any one

_____

Dreams and Visions

Key thought: Since Freud interpreted dreams as coming from the depths of man's subconscious, signifying his fears, anxieties, and suppressed desires, we have almost forgotten the possibility that God might take over the subconscious long enough to show a man something he might not see while conscious. In simpler times men assumed that dreams showed not the darkness of their own hearts but the light they needed.

1. Two closely interrelated dreams are recorded in Genesis 41. What are these dreams? _Dreams of skinny/fat cows ⅗ grains_

   What lifesaving plan of action resulted from heeding these dreams (vv. 33–36)? _Planned for the famine appointing Joseph, took over 1/5 of the land_

   Why was this plan of action so important to the well-being of the Israelites? (See Genesis 45:10–11; 50:20–21.) _It saved the Isrealites because they were not prepared_

2. Daniel 2 contains a record of a dream given to Nebuchadnezzar, king of Babylon. Nebuchadnezzar refused to reveal his dream to those he asked to interpret it. Why do you suppose he did this? _So he would know if they were telling the truth_

According to verse 11, what did the Babylonian wise men recognize about the origin of dreams? _it came from " gods "_

_____

_____

_____

When Daniel was brought in to interpret the dream, whom did he acknowledge as the giver of dreams (v. 28)? _God_

_____

_____

_____

_____

3. Acts 16:6–10 provides an interesting account of the way in which God provides guidance. What prevented Paul and his companions from preaching in Asia and Bithynia? _the Spirit of the Lord_

_____

_____

_____

How did God finally show Paul that he was to go to Macedonia? _a dream "vision of man from Macedonia"_

_____

_____

Macedonia was west of where Paul was at the time. Some scholars believe that had God allowed Paul to travel where *he* wanted to go, the gospel would have spread in an easterly rather than a westerly direction, and Asia, rather than Europe, would have been Christianized. Do you agree? Why or why not? _____

_____

_____

_____

Prophets

Key thought: How often we read this artless introduction in the Old Testament: "The word of the Lord came to me saying. . . ." We are not told how the word came, or how they knew it was the Lord who spoke, but it came, and they knew who was speaking, and they put down what he said.

1. According to 2 Peter 1:20–21, where does prophecy originate?
   From God through the Holy Spirit

2. First Peter 1:10–12 provides further information on the nature of prophecy. Do prophets always fully understand their message?
   No -

   Whom do prophets serve? *Us, future generations, God*

3. God frequently used prophets to provide guidance. One particularly interesting illustration of this is found in 2 Samuel 7:1–17. According to this passage, what did King David plan to do?
   Build a temple for the Ark.

What did the Lord reveal to Nathan, the prophet, and how did this change David's plan? _It was not David's job_

Did the Lord immediately reveal his will to Nathan? _____

What does this tell us about the importance of waiting on the Lord until he reveals his will to us? _____

Applying God's Truth to Your Life

1. Several instances of modern-day supernatural guidance are described on pages 68, 71–73. Have you ever experienced God's guidance through supernatural means? If so, describe your experience.

2. Whether or not you have experienced God's guidance through the supernatural means of dreams, prophecies, and the like, throughout your life God has guided you. Describe a recent occasion when you have been especially aware of God's guidance.

3. What is the most important lesson that you have learned from this study on supernatural guidance? _____

_____

_____

_____

To Do This Week

Pray that you will be especially sensitive to the means by which God is guiding you. Each day try to identify a way that God has provided guidance in your life.

STUDY SEVEN

the natural means

Read John 10:1–18

We are going along in life, doing the usual things, when suddenly we come up against a thing we are not sure about. We need guidance. The temptation is to stop everything and ask for a sign. Once in a while this is the thing to do. Gideon did it when he put out his fleece, asking that on the first night it should be wet with dew while the ground around remained dry and that the opposite should happen on the second night. But far more often we find God leading men while they are doing what they normally are supposed to do. When the Lord called them, David was taking care of sheep, the boy Samuel was serving in the temple, and Matthew was collecting taxes.

The author identifies ten natural means that God uses to guide us. They are duty, timing, God's calling you by name, human agents, gifts and abilities, desires, our frame of reference, circumstances, advice from friends, and being in a position where we must choose the harder of two things.

Duty

Key thought: "Do the next thing" is one of the best pieces of advice I have ever had. It works in any kind of situation and is especially helpful when we don't know what to do. What if we don't even know what the "next thing" is? We can find something. Some duty lies on our doorstep. The rule is DO IT. The doing of that thing may open our eyes to the next.

1. Read Ecclesiastes 12:13. According to this passage, what is your duty? _____
   _____
   _____
   _____

2. In Luke 17:7–10, Jesus puts duty in an interesting perspective. Summarize what he says. _____
   _____
   _____
   _____

3. List some of your daily duties. _____
   _____
   _____
   _____

   How is performing them a way of accepting God's guidance?
   _____
   _____
   _____
   _____
   _____

Timing

Key thought: God never showed me his will until the time came. I realize that nearly all of my trouble with finding out the will of God came because I wanted it too soon. I like to plan. I like to have things mapped out well in advance, and uncertainty of any sort puts me on edge. Perhaps it is for this very reason God has often asked me to wait until the last minute.

1. Describe a situation in your life when you were impatient to have the Lord reveal his will. _____

_____

_____

2. What happened when he finally revealed his will? _____

_____

_____

3. Could you see that his timing was better than yours? How?

_____

_____

_____

God Calls Us by Name

Key thought: We may not hear an audible voice, but we will find that the Lord knows how to call us. He knows the best way to get our attention, and if we are ready to listen or to be shown, we will hear or see whatever it is he has chosen as his means.

1. Deuteronomy 15:5 says in part to "carefully obey the voice of the LORD your God, to observe with care all [his] commandments" (NKJV). To what does this passage link hearing God's voice?

_____

_____

_____

Do you have to hear an audible voice to obey God's commands? _____

_____

_____

_____

2. What does Revelation 3:20 tell you to do when you hear the voice
   of the Lord? _____
   _____
   _____

Human Agents

Key thought: God guides his people always in relationship to
one another, like a flock. This is perhaps one of the most important
things to remember when we are looking for personal guidance. We
ought to look first of all to those with whom we have some special
relationship.

1. Read Philemon 8–16. How did God use Paul to persuade Philemon to do the right thing? _____
   _____
   _____
   _____

2. Study Romans 13:1–3. According to this passage, what is your
   duty to the civil authorities? _____
   _____
   _____
   _____

   How does God use governing authorities to show you the right
   thing to do? _____
   _____
   _____
   _____

3. Who are the most influential people in your life? _____
   _____
   _____
   _____

Gifts and Abilities

Key thought: When I am looking for the right direction, I ought to take into account what experience I have had, what gifts or propensities are mine, and what the direction of my life seems to have prepared me for.

1. Study Romans 12:3–8. According to this passage, what gifts are you to use? _____
   _____
   _____

   Write out verse 3. _____
   _____
   _____

   What does this verse mean to you? _____
   _____
   _____

2. Describe an occasion when you tried to do something for which you didn't have the proper abilities. _____
   _____
   _____
   _____

   What were the results? _____
   _____
   _____
   _____

3. How does your knowing what your gifts and abilities are allow God to guide you in your daily life? _____
   _____
   _____
   _____

Desires

Key thought: I may now and then actually want what God wants. This is likely to be the case more and more as I practice obedience, but it can also be a very simple and natural thing.

1. For a long time, I took the view that whatever I might want to do could not possibly be what God wanted me to do.

   This is a typical reaction among many Christians. Why do you suppose this is? _____
   _____
   _____
   _____

   Have you ever felt this way? _____
   _____
   _____
   _____

   If so, why? _____
   _____
   _____
   _____

2. Carefully study Psalm 37:4. Write out this verse. _____
   _____
   _____
   _____
   _____

   What condition does this verse place on receiving the desires of your heart? _____
   _____
   _____
   _____

Your Own Frame of Reference

Key thought: God leads me, I believe, within my own frame of reference. What I am, where I am, and how I got there, all have a great deal to do with what my frame of reference is. God can be counted on to choose the right avenue of approach.

1. What is a frame of reference? _____
   _____
   _____

   Briefly describe what yours is. _____
   _____
   _____
   _____

2. As a youth it hardly occurred to me that God needed to meet different people in different ways, or that his truth could take forms that would be unrecognizable to me.

   How might God guide, say, a Lebanese Christian in a way different from the way in which he guides you? _____
   _____
   _____

Circumstances

Key thought: If we try to trace what look to us like the significant events or turning points in any life, we will not go far before we find it was in the ordinary course that the extraordinary happened.

1. Read Romans 8:28. What does this verse say about the way God uses circumstances? *for his purpose*
   according to his will
   _____
   _____

2. The Bible is full of accounts of how God used circumstances to guide people and accomplish his will. One such account is found in Genesis 40–41. Where was Joseph when this story begins?

    In prison in Egypt
    _____
    _____

Who was in prison with him? _Cupbearer ?_
    baker
    _____
    _____
    _____

How did God use the imprisonment of Pharaoh's cupbearer to eventually release Joseph from prison and place him in a position of authority in Egypt? _it was Joseph's_
    link to Pharaoh
    _____
    _____

What does this tell you about the way God guides the lives of his people? _it is in His timing,_
    and our steps are ordered
    _____
    _____
    _____

3. Describe a situation in your own life when God used a set of circumstances to guide you in an unanticipated direction. _____
    _____
    _____
    _____
    _____

Advice from Friends

Key thought: It is a good thing to talk over a decision with a friend. The times we find ourselves entirely alone in making a decision are rare. Nearly always there are others who will be affected by what we decide, and usually some of these can be consulted.

1. Sometimes sound advice can avert tragedy. Read the account of David, Nabal, and Abigail in 1 Samuel 25. What advice did Abigail give David?_____

_____

_____

_____

_____

What positive effect did it have? _____

_____

_____

_____

_____

2. Not all advice is good advice. In 1 Kings 12:1–17 good advice was rejected and bad advice accepted. Briefly describe what happened.

_____

_____

_____

_____

Why do you suppose King Rehoboam chose to listen to such poor advice from his friends? _____

_____

_____

_____

_____

3. Describe an occasion when God used advice from a friend to help you make a wise decision. _____

_____

_____

_____

_____

4. How can you tell the difference between good and bad advice from a friend? _____

_____

_____

_____

The Harder of Two Things

Key thought: Sometimes we have narrowed down the possibilities to two, but there seems no way to choose one of them. Choose the harder of the two ways. If you have eliminated all other possibilities and there still seem to be two that might please God, choose the more difficult one.

1. When facing two alternatives, why is it important for you to choose the one that is more difficult? _____

_____

_____

_____

2. Describe an occasion when choosing the harder alternative turned out to be the better choice. _____

_____

_____

_____

Applying God's Truth to Your Life

1. List three important decisions you are presently facing. What means are available to help you make each of these decisions?

   a. _____

   b. _____

   c. _____

2. Describe a decision one of your friends is facing. Based on what you have learned in this study, what advice would you give in helping your friend make the right decision? _____

   _____

   _____

   _____

3. Of the ten natural means that God uses to help people make their decisions, which have you found most beneficial in the choices you have faced? _____

   _____

   _____

   _____

   Why did you find these to be the most beneficial? _____

   _____

   _____

   _____

To Do This Week

Identify the most difficult choice you are now facing. Each day pray that the Lord will make you aware of a particular means he is using to help you make that decision. As God reveals these means, be sure to thank him for his guidance in leading you to make the right decision.

notes

Introduction

1. Matthew 14:28–31
2. James 4:17 RSV
3. Matthew 19:16–22

Chapter 2 What Is Promised

1. Psalm 23:1
2. C. S. Lewis, *The Four Loves* (New York: Harcourt, Brace, 1960), 188.
3. James 1:17
4. Psalm 23:4
5. Genesis 2; Revelation 7:17 RSV
6. Isaiah 40:11 RSV
7. Isaiah 42:16 RSV
8. Isaiah 49:10 RSV
9. Isaiah 49:11 RSV
10. Isaiah 57:18 RSV
11. Psalm 56:13
12. Exodus 33:14

Chapter 3 The Conditions

1. Deuteronomy 31:8 RSV
2. Hebrews 3:17 PHILLIPS

3. John 14:9 NEB
4. Hebrews 11:6 RSV
5. Genesis 15:1 RSV
6. Genesis 28:13, 15 RSV
7. Exodus 3:6–8, 12 RSV
8. Daniel 4
9. Acts 9:5
10. Revelation 1:17–19 RSV
11. Exodus 5:2 RSV
12. Psalm 46:10
13. Joshua 10:13; 2 Kings 6:6; Psalm 48:14
14. Exodus 6:3 RSV margin
15. John 17:3 RSV
16. Hosea 6:3 RSV
17. Habakkuk 3:12, 13, 15, 19 RSV
18. Mark 9:20–25 RSV
19. Hebrews 11:1 RSV
20. Proverbs 10:17
21. Psalm 37:23
22. Psalm 25:9
23. Proverbs 11:3 RSV
24. Psalm 15:2–5 RSV
25. Isaiah 58:9–10 RSV
26. Matthew 16:24–25 RSV
27. Matthew 6:10 RSV
28. Matthew 10:37–38 RSV
29. C. S. Lewis, *Surprised by Joy* (New York: Harcourt, Brace, 1955), 229.
30. Graham Greene, *A Sort of Life* (New York: Simon & Schuster, 1971), 169.
31. Psalm 31:3
32. Isaiah 9:6 RSV; Exodus 17:15 RSV; Psalm 89:8, and elsewhere
33. Matthew 6:9 RSV
34. George MacDonald, "The Word of Jesus on Prayer," *Unspoken Sermons*, 2nd Series (London: Longmans, Green, and Co., 1885), p. 90; quoted in C. S. Lewis, *George MacDonald, An Anthology* (New York: The Macmillan Company, 1947), 53.
35. Matthew 7:24–27
36. 1 John 2:3 PHILLIPS
37. Hebrews 12:2 RSV; 5:8
38. Mark 14:33 PHILLIPS; Matthew 26:39

39. Psalm 48:14
40. 2 Timothy 1:12
41. Psalms 5:8; 25:5; 27:11; 31:3; 43:3; 61:2; 139:23–24; 143:10 RSV
42. Philippians 4:6
43. Philippians 4:6 PHILLIPS
44. Psalm 36:9
45. Romans 7:15–20 PHILLIPS
46. Romans 8:1–39
47. Luke 9:23 RSV
48. "A General Confession," *Book of Common Prayer.*
49. George MacDonald, "The Cause of Spiritual Stupidity," *Unspoken Sermons*, 2nd Series, pp. 59–61; quoted in C. S. Lewis, *George MacDonald, An Anthology*, 47.
50. Søren Kierkegaard, *Purity of Heart Is to Will One Thing*, trans. Douglas Steere (New York: Harper & Row, Harper Torchbook, 1956)
51. Deuteronomy 32:12
52. Hebrews 12:2–3 PHILLIPS

Chapter 4 The Objectives

1. John 14:6
2. Exodus 15:13 RSV
3. Romans 2:4 RSV
4. Luke 15:18
5. John 14:6
6. 1 Thessalonians 4:3 RSV
7. Exodus 15:17 RSV
8. Psalm 78:52 RSV
9. John 17:19
10. Hebrews 10:7
11. Matthew 4:1 RSV
12. 1 Kings 18, 19
13. 2 Kings 2:11
14. Psalm 23:3
15. Mark 7:31–37
16. Mark 8:22–26
17. Sir Robert Anderson, *The Silence of God* (Grand Rapids: Kregel, 1942), 171, 206.
18. Hebrews 2:10 RSV
19. Isaiah 58:11 RSV

20. Psalm 106:15
21. Matthew 8:20 RSV
22. Numbers 11:5 RSV
23. Psalm 44:18–19
24. Matthew 28:20, J. B. Rotherham, *The Emphasized Bible, A New Translation* (reprint ed., Grand Rapids: Kregel, 1968).
25. Hebrews 12:2
26. 1 Thessalonians 5:18 RSV
27. John 8:31–32, RSV
28. George MacDonald, "The Way," *Unspoken Sermons*, 2nd Series, 22; quoted in C. S. Lewis, *George MacDonald, An Anthology*, 42.
29. John 16:13 RSV
30. James 1:5
31. John 13:4–5 NEB

Chapter 5 The Means

1. Exodus 13:21 RSV
2. Exodus 40:36–37 RSV
3. Matthew 2:9–10 PHILLIPS
4. 2 Samuel 5:24 RSV
5. Acts 8:26 PHILLIPS
6. 2 Peter 2:8
7. Genesis 19:16 RSV
8. Daniel 2:27–28, 30 RSV
9. Acts 16:9–10 RSV; 22:17–21
10. 2 Chronicles 18
11. Jeremiah 38
12. Numbers 22
13. James 4:2
14. Deuteronomy 8:2, paraphrase
15. Mark 4:38 PHILLIPS
16. Joshua 3:15–16 RSV
17. The story has been told in *The Savage My Kinsman* (New York: Harper & Bros., 1960).
18. Deuteronomy 3:26, 27 RSV
19. Ruth 3:18
20. Habakkuk 2:1–4 RSV
21. John 10:3 RSV
22. John 20:14–16

23. Isaiah 43:1
24. John 10:4
25. John 21:21–22, literal
26. Ephesians 5:21; Romans 13:1–7; Ephesians 5:22; 6:1
27. Acts 5:29
28. Mark 7:13 RSV
29. Exodus 32:34 RSV
30. Psalm 77:19–20 RSV
31. Psalm 78:70–72 RSV
32. Exodus 4:2–9
33. John 2:1–11; 6:3–13; 9:1–7
34. 1 Corinthians 12:6 PHILLIPS
35. Romans 12:3 PHILLIPS
36. "A General Confession," *Book of Common Prayer.*
37. Psalm 139:14–15 RSV
38. Psalm 16:7 paraphrase
39. Proverbs 21:1
40. 1 Corinthians 10:27 PHILLIPS
41. Acts 16:6 NEB
42. Revelation 22:11 RSV
43. 1 Samuel 9:3 RSV
44. 1 Samuel 9:16 RSV
45. Romans 8:28 PHILLIPS
46. Psalm 32:8–9 RSV
47. Proverbs 3:5
48. Matthew 4:12–13 RSV
49. Matthew 5:1–2 RSV
50. Mark 14:12–16
51. Genesis 24:21 RSV
52. Genesis 24:27 RSV
53. "How Firm a Foundation," Richard Keen ("K" in John Ripon's Selections).
54. Matthew 18:19 RSV
55. Acts 1:24 RSV
56. Acts 20:22, 24 RSV
57. Acts 21:4 RSV
58. Galatians 1:16–17 RSV
59. 1 Kings 18:21 RSV
60. Hebrews 4:12–13 RSV
61. "The Son of God Goes Forth to War," Reginald Heber.

62. Matthew 7:14 RSV
63. Genesis 22
64. 1 Kings 8:18 RSV
65. Acts 16:7 RSV
66. Isaiah 30:21 RSV